THE GOOD D...

GUIDE TO...

BABY ON
A BUDGET

NOELLE WALSH

PAN BOOKS

First published 1995 by Pan Books
an imprint of Macmillan Publishers Limited
Cavaye Place, London SW10 9PG
and Basingstoke

Associated companies throughout the world

ISBN 0 330 34315 7

1 3 5 7 9 8 6 4 2

A CIP catalogue record for this book is available from
the British Library.

Typeset by Spottiswoode Ballantyne Printers Ltd, Colchester
Printed and bound in Great Britain by Cox & Wyman Ltd, Reading, Berkshire

CONTENTS

ACKNOWLEDGMENTS

With grateful thanks to my mother, Marrie, who no longer has young children to bring up, yet still treats every shopping trip as an opportunity to find a bargain. I thank her for those bargain-hunting genes. To parents everywhere whose shock at the sudden reduction in their standard of living will hopefully be offset by the information in this book. Enjoy your children without always counting the cost.

INTRODUCTION

Having a baby is an expensive business. Yes, it's also miraculous, fulfilling, joyous, awe-inspiring. But, distanced from the miracle of birth and the wonder of watching a new personality emerging, the practical considerations of rearing a family loom large.

Children are consummate consumers: even before they are born they are the impetus for trips to the shops to spend a small fortune on anything from nappies and baby cream, babygros and blankets to prams and alarms, cots and car seats. Then, as they grow up, there's the babywalker to help them to take their first steps, the first doll's house or train set, the garden swing, then the school uniform, sports equipment, trainers, computer games and the never-ending supply of clothes.

For parents, there is the awful realisation that all this money is not being spent on items that will be used until they have reached the end of their useful life. Babygros will be grown out of before an infant has even worn some of them; prams will be given up in favour of pushchairs and buggies within a few short months; doll's houses and train sets will make way for computers and CD-Roms; school uniforms – well, there's only so much hem on trousers and skirts.

So after spending thousands of pounds on juvenile paraphernalia, a significant amount of it will be disposed of when it's still in good condition. Not like the broken down washing machine which you arrange to have taken away because even your friendly electrician says it will never spin again.

Most parents will remember the day when they decided the family was big enough but the house wasn't and all those bags of baby clothes – still in pristine condition, some unworn – would have to go. Or the day when the youngest child grew out of the oldest child's handed-down bike and you gave it to the next door neighbour just to clear the space.

Informal handing on of clothes and equipment to others who

now need it has been going on for centuries. But the recent recession has made many people question whether they can still continue to hand on without any financial recompense. It has also increased the numbers of parents who can't always afford the as-new price.

That's why there are now hundreds of outlets around the country which sell good condition nearly-new baby and children's clothes and equipment. It's one of the few growth areas in retail during the recession. Some of these shops cater mainly for adult women and stock children's items as a sideline; others are aimed specifically at the children's market. However, most shops will admit that after the age of about eight, boys' secondhand clothes are hard to come by – boys tend to wear them out at this stage in their lives!

Equipment ranges from cots to prams – high expense items which aren't used for long. In the case of cots, it's best to buy a new mattress for the frame. Car seats are another item often offered in nearly-new shops: secondhand car seats are fine as long as they haven't been involved in an accident, even a minor bump. If you don't feel confident about this possibility, then don't risk it. Try Kwik Fit instead, many of whose branches will sell you a car seat, fit it and then take it back when you have finished with it and refund your money it it is still in good condition. The other problem with buying secondhand car seats is that they are rarely accompanied by the instructions which are important to ensure that the seat is properly installed. Some seats carry instructions on their rear or side panels – check that out first. Many seats now have removable, washable covers so if the seat is simply grubby, that is easily remedied.

Many of the outlets in this book are factory shops. If you consider the plethora of children's clothes in the high street shops and department stores, you can imagine how many factories are busy making all these garments. What are you getting when you visit a factory shop? Some of the stock is made up of seconds: quality control is now so stringent that even the most minuscule of flaws is relegated to the seconds division. Moreover, machines set on a certain run may cut more garment parts than are required to make up an order, so these become overmakes or overproduction. Some factories also still operate on the traditional 'cabbage' basis, when they are allowed to take a percentage of the run to sell themselves, as long as they don't label the garments with a store's name. So customers are getting a perfect garment, made in exactly the same way as those with the store's label were made, but at a lower price.

For those who haven't visited a factory shop, they vary enormously: some are still situated in a building on the factory site; others look just like a high street shop, with changing rooms and window displays. What they all offer is the chance to buy brand-name – though sometimes unlabelled – products at prices which are between 15% and 80% less than high street prices.

Of course, you won't be able to walk into a factory shop and buy exactly the same item as is on sale in the high street at exactly the same time, at least not if it's perfect quality. Most of the merchandise in factory shops is what is called 'end of season' stock. But bear in mind that shop seasons and nature's seasons do not run in parallel. When the shops are stocking summer T-shirts and shorts in late February and you're still trying to find long trousers and sweaters for your growing clan in what can still be bitter weather, you will find them in factory shops. Later, perhaps in May, you will then find the summer T-shirt and shorts in factory shops as high street shops prepare for their summer sales.

The other big expense with children is their rooms. Even if you don't decorate a room specifically as the nursery, as they get older, children start making demands about how they want their room to look which usually involves some expense. This book will tell you where to go to find discount fabric, secondhand top-quality curtains, new carpets and furniture to save you money when the inevitable happens.

Bringing up a family also involves peripheral expense. You tend to find that all your friends have children at around the same time, so you end up buying lots of christening, birthday and Christmas presents for dozens of children whose names you struggle to remember but with whose parents you shared your first hangover. So this book also contains outlets where you can find many traditional gifts at discount prices. Again, some of these items are infinitesimally flawed seconds; others are old stock which needs to be cleared in order to make way for new designs. But when these gifts consist of silver goblets or napkin rings, the fact that they are last year's design won't be of major concern.

Once upon a time, it was considered not the done thing to use secondhand (now renamed nearly-new) shops and factory outlets. Now, it is regarded as a positive virtue to seek out value for money. What began as a way to help combat the recession has become a way of life. People who in the Eighties would think nothing of splashing out on clothes and toys for their children, now practise thrift and preach the art of self-denial.

That doesn't mean to say life isn't fun any more, that retail therapy has lost its force. Shopping for bargains is even more fun than ordinary high street, full-price shopping. To leave a shop knowing you have bought something you really wanted or needed and saved money – that's really exciting.

Opportunities for everyone to save money on their purchases are going to grow over the next decade. The last five years has seen a rapid increase in the numbers of nearly-new outlets; the next five will see a similar rise in the numbers of factory shopping centres in the United Kingdom.

Factory shopping centres consist of a cluster of factory shops, all selling discounted goods to the public. Until December 1994, there were only two such villages in Britain: Hornsea Freeport in East Yorkshire and Clarks in Street, Somerset. Just before Christmas 1994, Jacksons Landing opened in Hartlepool, selling at least twenty leading brands among the shops on site. For the family, these included JoKids childrenswear (which is also on sale at Clarks Village) and Toy World, which features many of the leading brand names such as Tomy, Fisher-Price and Lego.

As we were going to press, there were dozens of other such villages planned – though how many of them will eventually become reality is not yet known. Many of them are joint developments with American companies with experience of factory villages in the States. Look out for developments in Bicester, Swindon, Cheshire Oaks off junction 10 of the M53, Kendal in Cumbria, and Fleetwood in Lancashire.

Finally, some tips about bargain-hunting. First, and most important, never travel a long distance to a factory shop or nearly-new outlet without ringing them up first. They may have moved, gone out of business, changed their opening hours or simply not have a lot of stock in at the time you are thinking of visiting. Unlike high street shops, they don't know what they are going to be stocking from week to week and sometimes have sparse periods. Secondly, visit regularly and make friends with the owners or managers of your local nearly-new shops. You can make one visit and find nothing you like while a second will yield all sorts of delights. Once your face becomes known, you can discuss specific purchases and they may phone you up if an item comes in which you are looking for. This is particularly true of secondhand curtain shops. The Curtain Exchange outlets, for example, will not only phone you if something suitable comes in, they will also let you take the curtains or blinds home and let you hang them to see if you still like them before they bank your cheque. Thirdly, don't be put off by appearances. Some of these outlets may not look very exciting from the outside and even the inside may leave something to be desired – if you want excitement, check out the price tags! You should find it easy to seek out shops in your locality: the book is set out geographically so that you can immediately flick to your area – whether you are looking for clothes, curtains, cots or christening gifts.

Bringing up a family is a hard enough task without also involving financial difficulties. I hope this book helps you to make some significant savings and use that money to enjoy life and enjoy your children – before you know it, they will have grown up and gone.

Noelle Walsh

A NOTE ABOUT REGIONS

Within the various chapters, for ease of reference, the UK has been divided into the following regions:

LONDON
Including Greater London.

SOUTH EAST
Including Buckinghamshire, Bedfordshire, Hertfordshire, Essex, Kent, East Sussex, West Sussex, Hampshire and the Isle of Wight, Berkshire, Surrey.

SOUTH WEST
Including Cornwall, Devon, Somerset, Dorset, Wiltshire, Avon.

WALES AND WEST MIDLANDS
Including Clwyd, Gwynedd, Dyfed, Powys, West Glamorgan, Mid Glamorgan, Gloucestershire, Oxfordshire, Warwickshire, West Midlands, Staffordshire, Shropshire, Hereford and Worcester.

EAST ANGLIA AND EAST MIDLANDS
Including Norfolk, Suffolk, Cambridgeshire, Northampton-shire, Leicestershire, Lincolnshire, Nottinghamshire, Derby-shire.

NORTH WEST, YORKSHIRE AND HUMBERSIDE
Including Lancashire, Merseyside, Cheshire, Greater Manches-ter, West Yorkshire, South Yorkshire, Humberside, North Yorkshire.

NORTH AND SCOTLAND
Including Cumbria, Durham, Cleveland, Tyne and Wear, Northumberland, Dumfries and Galloway, Strathclyde, Loth-ian, Central, Fife, Tayside, Grampian, Highlands and Islands.

NORTHERN IRELAND

CLOTHING AND FOOTWEAR

LONDON

BURBERRY

29-33 CHATHAM PLACE, LONDON E9 6LP
☎ 0181-985 3344. OPEN 12.30 – 6 MON – FRI, 9.30 – 1 SAT.
Most of the Burberry factory shops sell seconds and overmakes of the famous name raincoats and duffle coats, as well as accessories such as the distinctive umbrellas, scarves and handbags, plus gift food items. All carry the Burberry label and are about one third of the normal retail price. Childrenswear tends to be thin on the ground, so phone before visiting.

CHANGE OF HABIT

25 ABBEVILLE ROAD, LONDON SW4 9LA
☎ 0181-675 9475. OPEN 11 – 5 MON – FRI, 10 – 6 SAT.
Nearly-new clothes for babies and children up to the age of 10, as well as women's nearly-new. Also has mother-to-be wear, prams, cots, baby walkers, party clothes, and children's bedding.

CHANGE OF HEART

59 PARK ROAD, CROUCH END, LONDON N8
☎ 0181-341 1575. OPEN 10 – 6 MON – SAT, 10 – 5 WED, CLOSED THUR.
Primarily a lady's dress agency, they also offer nearly-new childrenswear, but no equipment or footwear, from birth to three years. Mostly designer labels, there are lots of French labels including Oilily, OshKosh and Petit Bateau.

If you're pregnant, don't forget that you are eligible for free dental treatment and prescriptions up to one year after the birth of your baby. You'll also be given free booklets on parenthood by your health visitor or ante natal clinic.

CHEEKY MONKEYS

202 KENSINGTON PARK ROAD, LONDON W11 1NR
☎ 0171-792 9022. OPEN 9.30 – 5.30 MON – FRI,
10 – 5.30 SAT.

A mixture of secondhand and new in this shop aimed specifically at parents. Secondhand babies' and children's clothes and equipment, including prams, high chairs, stair gates, car seats, baby bouncers. Nearly-new children's clothes include Oilily and OshKosh. Also, new toys, Start-Rite shoes professionally fitted, gifts, stickers, books, tapes, Playdoh, Tomy goods, safety products and hairdressing.

DESIGNS

60 ROSSLYN HILL, LONDON NW3 1ND
☎ 0171-435 0100. OPEN 10 – 5.45 MON – SAT, UNTIL 6.45 ON THUR.

Designs has been established for twelve years, selling ladies' designer clothes and accessories, but they now also stock a range of children's clothes from 0–8 years. The selection is small and for girls only.

You can get a free 128-page pregnancy guide called *Emma's Diary* from your GP as soon as your pregnancy is confirmed. Published for the Royal College of General Practitioners by Lifecycle Marketing, *Emma's Diary* takes you through pregnancy; with helpful advice and includes a claim card for a free gift pack from branches of Boots or Children's World. Your GP or midwife can get free supplies of *Emma's Diary* by writing to RCGP, *Emma's Diary*, Freepost (No SL1 313), Maidenhead, Berks SL6 7YA, or by phoning 01628 771232. Copies can only be supplied to registered GP surgery addresses.

HANGERS

120 PITSHANGER LANE, EALING, LONDON W5 1QP
☎ 0181-810 9363. OPEN 10-6 MON – SAT.
Primarily a women's dress agency, it also stocks a very small selection of boys' and girlswear from 12 months to eight years and ranging from Marks & Spencer to designer labels.

JUST OUTGROWN

99 DEVONSHIRE ROAD, CHISWICK, LONDON W4
☎ 0181-995 5405. OPEN 10 – 4 TUE – FRI, 10 – 1 SAT.
Secondhand children's clothes and equipment with seasonal bargain rails.

RAINBOW

249 & 253 ARCHWAY ROAD, LONDON N6
☎ 0181-340 8003. OPEN 10.30 – 5 MON, 10.30 – 5.30 TUE – SAT.
Number 249 sells secondhand items, while 253 is new merchandise. Nearly-new consists of a wide range of well-known baby and children's clothes – from OshKosh and Oilily to Baby Gap and Marks & Spencer – as well as good condition baby equipment from cots and high chairs to car seats and playpens. They also sell secondhand toys (Galt and Fisher-Price), including a lot of traditional wooden toys such as Brio wooden trains, and books. The new shop sells a wide range of children's clothes, mainly in natural fabrics, and the imported items are discounted by about $12\frac{1}{2}\%$. There are twice-yearly sales in January and July when prices are discounted further.

Buy a child's car seat from Kwik Fit and if returned in good condition, your money will be refunded. This is particularly useful for parents who opt for a car seat which only lasts until their baby is about nine months old, rather than a seat which can be used until the age of four or five, by which time it will almost certainly be too grubby to exchange. Check Yellow Pages for your local supplier.

SCARECROW

131 WALHAM GREEN COURT, MOORE PARK ROAD, LONDON
SW6 2DG

☎ 0171-381 1023. OPEN 10 – 5 TUE – FRI, 9.30 – 1 SAT.

London's biggest and probably best-known children's dress
agency, Scarecrow offers two floors of hardly-worn clothes
including popular designer labels such as Oilily and Harrods,
and caters for all ages from babyhood to 18 years. As well as the
more traditional rompers, smocked dresses and velvet-collared
coats, there are dinner jackets and party frocks alongside jeans,
checked shirts and sweatshirts. There is also an extensive range
of sports clothes which include karate suits, ski wear, riding and
sailing gear, plus the appropriate footwear.

SWALLOWS & AMAZONS

91 NIGHTINGALE LANE, LONDON SW12 8NX

☎ 0181-673 0275. OPEN 10 – 5 MON – SAT.

Swallows & Amazons, now more than a decade old, is the
largest secondhand children's shop in South London. Quality
clothes for 0–12 year olds include Jacardi, Oilily, Jean le
Bourget, OshKosh and Gap, as well as an Aladdin's cave in the
basement of toys, books, and baby equipment and a play area.
Due to demand, they now stock new travel cots, playpens and
umbrella buggies at very competitive prices. Children's hairdressing is very popular and available most afternoons
(appointments necessary). There is a huge variety of constantly
changing stock. You are always welcome to come and browse,
whether buying or selling.

Buy new and secondhand books in good condition at sales held by
Amnesty International's British Section. Normally, a local Amnesty group
hires a hall and sets up stall with thousands of books on sale, many of
them publishers' review copies. Look up the telephone number of your local
Amnesty branch in the business telephone directory for your area and
check when the sale is on.

THE BABY'S ROOM

173 St John's Hill, Wandsworth, London SW11
☎ 0171-924 4711. Open 10 – 6 Mon – Sat, 11 – 3 Sun.
Specialising in secondhand equipment for infants and tiny tots up to the age of three, there is also a small selection of clothing of labels such as Marks & Spencer, Next, Gap and Jonelle.

THE BEST OF SECONDHAND

42 Golders Green Road, London NW11
☎ 0181-458 3890. Open 9.30 – 5.30 Mon – Fri, 9.30 – 6 Sat, 10 – 5 Sun.
Primarily a dress agency selling top designer names and middle of the range labels, there is now also a small selection of children's party dresses.

THE BRAND CENTRE

Mollison Avenue, Stockingswater Lane, Brimsdown, Enfield, Middlesex EN3 7PH
☎ 0181-805 8080. Open 10 – 8 Mon – Fri, 10 – 7 Sat, 10 – 6 Sun.
The fashion equivalent of the US warehouse-style super supermarkets in that it offers out-of-town location, plenty of free car parking and brand name goods at discount prices. In the case of The Brand Centre, a 40,000 sq ft warehouse, most of the stock is designer names for men and women, but there are some children's lines. Discounts average about 25% by working on high turnover and low profit margins. Phone first to check children's stock.

> Wear a perfume constantly while nursing the new baby in hospital and continue to wear the same fragrance after you get home. Then when you put the baby to bed, you can put a drop of that perfume on the sheet or mattress (never put a pillow in a baby's cot) and the baby will associate the smell with you, giving you an increased chance of an unbroken's night's sleep.

TUTTI FRUTTI DISCOUNT STORE

156-158 RYE LANE, PECKHAM, LONDON SE15 4NB
☎ 0171-732 9933. OPEN 9 – 6 MON – SAT.
Nursery equipment shop which offers bigger discounts the
more you buy and particularly if you pay cash. There are often
special offers – buggies from £20, cots for £100. They stock all
leading makes, as well as babywear, shoes, baby accessories,
bedding, bath sets, textiles, feeding equipment, and have a
repair service and a mail order facility. There are baby changing
facilities in the shop and toys to play with.

WINKIE JANE

184 MUNSTER ROAD, FULHAM, LONDON SW6 6AU
☎ 0171-384 1762. OPEN 9 – 5.30 MON – FRI, 10 – 5 SAT.
Good quality nearly-new children's clothing in this very child-
friendly shop with its big double doors for easy access with
buggies and a toy box for children to play with while parents
browse. There is on-street parking right outside and the clothes
are well presented and uncluttered. Stock constantly changes
and includes designers such as Oilily, Jacardi, Chicaloo,
OshKosh, David Charles and Heather Brown. Age range
covered is 0–10. There are also car seats, buggies, prams,
wooden toy boxes, Designers Guild quilts, baby Dior samples
and unwanted gifts, as new.

Most new mothers receive a Bounty Pack when they are in hospital after
giving birth. This contains samples and sometimes even full-size packs of a
wide range of products from baby lotion, wipes and shampoo to nappy
sacks, toothpaste, nappies and photographic discounts. It's useful for trying
out products before deciding whether they suit you and your baby. The new
mother pack also contains a Babycare book which has a claim card which
you can redeem at Boots the Chemist for a Baby Progress Pack when your
child is four months. This gives you products appropriate to your baby's
age such as baby food, drink, rusks, powdered meals, etc. The mothers of
more than 800,000 babies a year receive these packs.

SOUTH EAST

BARGAIN BOUTIQUE
SNOW HILL, CRAWLEY DOWN, WEST SUSSEX RH10 3EE
☎ (01342) 712022. OPEN 9.15 – 2.15 TUE – SAT.
BB caters mainly for women and children with labels such as
Marks & Spencer, Laura Ashley, Next and Oilily at one quarter to
one third of the original price. There is no underwear or footwear
and toddlers' clothes only range from about three years.

BARNADO'S
94 HIGH STREET, ROCHESTER, KENT ME1 1JT
☎ (01634) 831843. OPEN 9 – 5 MON – SAT.
Everything secondhand from clothes from birth to 14 years, to
toys. There is a toy fair every year – ring for details.

BENJAMIN'S MESS
77 HIGH STREET, ROCHESTER KENT ME1 1LX
☎ (01634) 817848. OPEN 9 – 5.30 MON – SAT.
This shop sells women's and children's clothes mainly, from
babywear up to the age of ten. Mainly dresses, shirts, coats and
jackets with labels such as Levi's, Oilily, OshKosh. There is a
limited amount of footwear.

BLOOMING MARVELLOUS
6 MOUNT PARADE, MOUNT PLEASANT ROUNDABOUT,
COCKFOSTERS, BARNET HERTS EN4 9DD
☎ 0181-441 5582. 10 – 5 MON – SAT.
The Blooming Marvellous shop sells childrenswear for 0–11
year olds, co-ordinating womenswear and maternity wear and
is only eight minutes from junction 24 of the M25. It stocks the
same range as the catalogue and also sells samples, ends of lines
and seconds. All the childrenswear is exclusive to Blooming
Marvellous and is designed in bright, practical fabrics that are
machine washable.

BUMPSADAISY

BROMPTON WALK, LAKESIDE SHOPPING COMPLEX,
SOUTH THURROCK, ESSEX RM16 1ZL
☎ (01708) 890121. PHONE FOR OPENING TIMES.
33 WEST STREET, MARLOW, ESSEX
☎ (01628) 478487. PHONE FOR OPENING TIMES.
Franchised hire shops with large range of special occasion
maternity wear, from wedding outfits to ball gowns, to hire
and to buy. Hire costs average about £30 for special occasion
wear. Phone 0171-379 9831 for details of your local stockist.

C A WILLIAMS

87-91 TAVISTOCK STREET, BEDFORD, BEDFORDSHIRE
☎ (01234) 354657. OPEN 8.30 – 6 MON – SAT.
Seconds of Doc Martens at half price, and perfects and seconds
of Wranglers jeans and tops at discount for eight year olds
upwards.

CANCER RESEARCH GROUP

172 TERMINUS ROAD, EASTBOURNE,
EAST SUSSEX BN21 3SB
☎ (01323) 739703. OPEN 9.30 – 4.30 MON – SAT.
Shop specifically aimed at the bridal market which also sells
outfits for pageboys and bridesmaids' dresses.

School project material can be found free if you know where to look. If your
child is studying tea producing areas or nutrition you can get free leaflets
from the Tea Council and many of the supermarkets and manufacturers.
Contact the Tea Council for colourful posters telling where tea comes from
and how it is harvested on 0171-248 1024. Sainsbury's supermarket has a
freephone student line on 0800 387504. Tesco runs a Careline on 0800
505555. John West Foods Ltd sends out information packs – write to the
Marketing Department at West House, Bixteth Street, Liverpool L3 9SR or
phone (0151) 236 8771.

CLEARANCE CENTRE

78-82 HIGH STREET, SUTTON, SURREY SM1 1EF
☎ 0181-770 9770. OPEN 9 – 5.30 MON – FRI, 9 – 6 SAT.
Allders department store has a special clearance centre in its old shop just down the road from Sutton station. Operating under the name of Clearance Centre, rather than Allders, the centre sells clearance lines of the same sort of children's clothes you would find in the department store, but no baby equipment or toys. Don't confuse the discount centre with the Allders store in the St. Nicholas Shopping Centre.

COSTCO

WEST THURROCK WAY, WEST THURROCK,
ESSEX RM16 1WY
☎ (01708) 860557. OPEN 10 – 8.30 MON – FRI, 9 – 6.30 SAT, 11 – 5 SUN.
HARTSPRING LANE, BUSHEY, WATFORD,
HERTFORDSHIRE WD2 8JS
☎(01923) 225449. OPEN AS ABOVE.
A members-only discount warehouse, specialising in food but also selling everything from computers and TVs, washing machines and cameras to books and clothes. There is plenty here for hard-pressed parents. Apart from the savings on tins of baked beans and fish fingers, there are children's clothes and discounted books, plus computer games and other electronic equipment for older offspring. You have to be VAT-registered or a member of a certain profession to join, although this is not a cash & carry and is open to individual members of the public. Phone head office on (01923) 213113 for membership details.

For ideas about places to visit on family outings, visit your local tourist board or tourist information office where there are usually scores of leaflets and booklets about your area. They are often useful education tools, too, as they offer historical and geographical information which you can pass onto your children on the spot.

DAISY DAISY

33 NORTH ROAD, BRIGHTON, EAST SUSSEX BN1 1YB
☎ (01273) 689108. OPEN 10 – 5 MON – SAT.
Dress agency aimed at children. Most of the stock is designer
label nearly-new outfits, as well as some high street names for
children at between one quarter and one half of the original
price. Labels include Oilily, OshKosh and Nipper as well as
well-known French and Italian designers. High street names
featured include Laura Ashley and Benetton. There are also
plenty of accessories including shoes, hats, socks, tights and
swimwear. The selection for newborn babies is large and there's
a playroom, nappy changing and a toilet, but no baby
equipment on sale.

DEJA VU

OLD SEAL HOUSE, 19 CHURCH STREET, SEAL,
NEAR SEVENOAKS, KENT TN15 0DA
☎ (0732) 762155. OPEN 10 – 4.30 MON – SAT.
Small range of nearly-new children's traditional smocked
dresses and jodphurs, and, from September each year, ski wear
for adults and children.

GOOSEBERRY BUSH

2 BARNHAM ROAD, BARNHAM, NR BOGNOR REGIS,
WEST SUSSEX PO22 0ES
☎ (01243) 554552 OPEN 10 – 4 MON – SAT
Nearly-new, largely high street fashions for the mother and
child, ie Next, Heskia and Mothercare. Stock ranges from a
good selection of maternity wear, children's wellingtons,
slippers and tracksuits to children's cots, toys, bedding and high
chairs. New items can be found for very reasonable prices.
Caters for children 0–10 years. Friendly atmosphere and said to
be a particular favourite with grandparents.

Never leave plastic bags lying around where children can reach them.

HEIRLOOMS LTD

2 ARUN BUSINESS PARK, BOGNOR REGIS,
WEST SUSSEX PO22 9SX
☎ (01243) 820252. OPEN ONCE A MONTH, USUALLY
10 – 5 ON THE FIRST FRIDAY AND SOME SUNS AND BANK
HOLIDAYS. PHONE FIRST FOR A LIST OF OPEN DAY DATES.
Traditional christening robes and baby clothes up to the age of
six, hand-embroidered with lace, and perfect for weddings and
parties. Silver and gold plated teddy bear picture frames,
napkin rings and other christening gifts, plus nursery bed
linens. Prices are anything from 18%–60% off the recommended retail price for slight seconds or perfect merchandise since
you are buying directly from the manufacturer.

KID2KID

2 THE HIGH STREET, COOKHAM, BERKSHIRE SL6 1SQ
☎ (01628) 531804. OPEN 10 – 5 MON – SAT.
Retail outlet selling nearly-new designer clothes for children
0–10 years. Some of the most popular designer labels include
Oilily, Cacheral, Ozona, Jean Bourget, Poivre Blanc, and
OshKosh, although quality items from Next, Marks & Spencer
and Laura Ashley are also on sale. Prices range from £5 to £30,
normally at least one-third of the original price. There is also
footwear – slippers, wellingtons, trainers and party shoes –
though not everyday shoes. Own range of new children's
taffeta partywear also available.

BEBE CONFORT
☎ (01732) 740880.

As a manufacturer, Bebe Confort does not sell direct to the public, but it
does supply some shops with ends of lines. Finding these shops can be a
time-consuming business. First, phone head office on the telephone
number given above and ask for the names of your local stockists. You
then have to phone round the stockists and ask if they have any end of
season lines or discontinued ranges.

MATALAN

UNIT 4B, THE TUNNEL ESTATE, WESTERN AVENUE,
LAKESIDE RETAIL PARK, WEST THURROCK,
ESSEX RM16 1HH
☎ (01708) 864350. OPEN 10 – 8 MON – FRI, 9 – 6 SAT,
11 – 5 SUN.
UNIT 4, RIVERSIDE RETAIL PARK, VICTORIA ROAD,
CHELMSFORD, ESSEX EM2 6LL
☎ (01245) 348787. OPEN 10 – 8 MON – FRI, 9 – 6 SAT,
11 – 5 SUN.
ROSE KILN LANE, OFF BASINGSTOKE ROAD, READING,
BERKSHIRE RG2 0SN
☎ (01734) 391958. OPEN 10 – 8 MON – FRI, 9 – 6 SAT,
11 – 5 SUN.
WATLING STREET, BLETCHLEY, MILTON KEYNES, MK1 1HS
☎ (01908) 373735. OPEN 10 – 8 MON – FRI, 9 – SAT,
11 – 5 SUN.

A former cash and carry company, Matalan has now become a
discount club operation which sells 90% clothing and 10%
household items, toiletries and luggage. Members are usually
employees whose company is registered with Matalan, senior
citizens with a pension through one of the listed companies, or
anyone who is VAT-registered. But members of the public can
gain access with a day pass. Merchandise is sold at between
20%–50% cheaper than high street prices. And unlike many
discount club operations, you don't have to buy in bulk. There's
a wide range of children's clothing including jeans, denim
jackets, coats, girls' dresses, jumpers and jogging suits, with
more merchandise for babies and children under 9, although
the age range does go up to about 12.

If you're planning a fund-raising event, your local branch of McDonalds will
supply free orange juice on a stand manned by a staff member. This can
be used either as free refreshment or sold to raise cash. Contact your local
branch manager for details and booking.

MEXX INTERNATIONAL

132-133 FAIRLIE ROAD, SLOUGH TRADING ESTATE,
SLOUGH, BERKSHIRE SL1 4PY
☎ (01753) 525450. OPEN 9.30 – 5.30 MON – SAT, UNTIL
7 ON THUR, 10 – 4 SUN.

High street fashion at factory outlet prices. On sale are Mini
Mexx for 0–2 year olds, Boy Kid and Girl Kid for 2–8 year olds,
Boy Teen and Girl Teen for 8–16 year olds. There are usually at
least 6,000 items in stock, with regular new deliveries, all of
which are heavily discounted by between 40%–80%. Merchandise is either samples, or from bankrupt retailers. The outlet can
be found by turning down off the Slough Farnham Road at Do It
All and turning right at the second set of traffic lights.

SMARTIES

4 STAMFORD SQUARE, OFF WARWICK STREET, WORTHING,
SUSSEX BN11 3EZ
☎ (01903) 23361. OPEN 10 – 5 MON – SAT.

Nearly-new shop selling quality high street – Marks & Spencer
– and designer labels such as OshKosh, Oilily, Pretty Boy for
children from birth to nine years of age. There is usually a good
range of babygros, dresses, trousers, jumpers and coats, boots,
shoes, trainers and riding boots, but no toys or nursery
equipment.

BOOTS THE CHEMIST
BRANCHES COUNTRYWIDE.
☎ (0800) 622 525.

Any parent who's staggered home with the weekly shopping and the
nappies will jump at the chance to have them delivered free. Boots the
Chemist will transport nappies to your home as long as you buy one
month's supply. You can either order and pay at your local store or phone
the free nappy home delivery service number above.

TATTERS

23 WEST STREET, RINGWOOD, HAMPSHIRE BH24 1DY
☎ (01425) 478511. OPEN 10 – 4 MON – FRI, CLOSED 1
WED, SAT.

As good as new clothes for women, with childrenswear
between the ages of 1 and 13 years, as well as a hiring service for
travel cots, high chairs and car seats.

THE FACTORY SHOP

UNIT 4C, THE GLOUCESTERS, LUCKYN LANE, BASILDON,
ESSEX SS14 3AX
☎ (01268) 520446. OPEN 9 – 5.30 MON – SAT, 10 – 5
SUN.

Large warehouse carrying a wide range of almost everything
you can imagine, most of which is overmakes, bankrupt stock,
discontinued lines and clearances. Stock changes daily and
there are always bargains to be found. There are branded toys
(Matchbox, Playskool) plus toiletries, soft toys, children's
partywear, and party gear such as balloons and banners.

THE FACTORY SHOP (ESSEX) LTD

THE GLOUCESTERS, LUCKYN LANE, PIPPS HILL INDUSTRIAL
ESTATE, BASILDON, ESSEX SS14 3AX
☎ (01268) 520446. OPEN 9 – 5.30 MON – SAT, 10 – 5
SUN.

No-frills factory shop selling seconds, discontinued lines and
some perfect current stock from many department and chain
store high street names. This is not the place to look for high
fashion, but it has an enormous amount of middle of the range
children's clothes, as well as bedlinen, towels, toys, sportswear,
within its 7,000 square feet of selling space. Everything is sold at
between 30% and 50% of the original price. Parking is easy, the
M25 is near and there's good wheelchair/pushchair access.

THE JEANS FACTORY

MOTOWN YARD, LONDON ROAD, STANFORD-LE-HOPE,
ESSEX
☎ (01375) 675643. OPEN 9 – 5 MON – FRI, 9 – 1 SAT.
Manufactures denim jeans for retail outlets and sells its own
label jeans at half price in its factory shop. It also sells denim
jackets from a sister factory which it supplies with denim and
Motown jeans. All are perfect and there is a small selection in
children's sizes from the age of six upwards. Prices start at £15.

THE SHOE SHED

C/O CLOTHING WORLD, ORCHARD ROAD, ROYSTON,
HERTS SG8 5HA
☎ (01763) 241933. OPEN 10 – 6 TUE, WED, 10 – 8 THUR,
FRI, 10 – 4 SAT, 10 – 2 SUN.
Wide range of quality footwear at below retail prices. There are
no seconds – just perfects, as you would expect from a high
street store. They stock a variety of brand names such as Dunlop
and for very young babies trying their first shoes, Dandystepps.
Sizes start from 2 and prices from £4.50. They also stock their
own quality shoes, The Jennings Collection – prices start from
£7.50 – and their Reflex range of sports shoes. Staff are friendly
and willing to help.

THE STOCK EXCHANGE

1-3 HIGH STREET, SUNNINGHILL, ASCOT,
BERKSHIRE SL5 5NQ
☎ (01344) 25420. OPEN 9 – 5.30 MON – FRI, 9 – 4.30
SAT.
Whole section of childrenswear – everything from jumpers to
coats – in this general dress agency, but no underwear,
nightwear or footwear.

Before removing a child's plaster, rub it with cotton wool dipped in baby oil
– it won't hurt them so much.

SOUTH WEST

BUDGET-BOX
24A DITTON ST, ILMINSTER, SOMERSET TA19 0BQ
☎ (01460) 53316. OPEN 9 – 5 MON – WED & FRI, 9 – 1
THUR & SAT.
Nearly-new childrenswear up to early teens stocked, including
OshKosh, and school uniforms suitable for the local schools in
this dress agency which primarily caters for women.

CHILD'S PLAY
28 ALBION STREET, EXMOUTH, DEVON EX8 1JJ
☎ (01395) 276975. OPEN 10 – 4 MON, TUE, THUR – SAT,
10 – 1 WED, CLOSED 1 – 2 DAILY.
Secondhand and new baby equipment and clothes for ages 0–6
years. Babygros cost from 50p to £2.99; prams from £5 to £100.

CLARKS FACTORY SHOPPING VILLAGE
STREET, SOMERSET BA16 0YA
☎ (01458) 42131. OPEN 9 – 6 MON – SAT, 11 – 5 SUN.
Three dozen factory outlet shops selling mainly ends of lines,
overmakes and seconds at discounts of up to 60%. Most of the
outlets are for adults, but there is a JoKids shop and the Clarks
outlet has plenty of children's shoes, slippers, wellingtons,
boots and trainers. The Clarks Sports Factory Shop sells
clothing and equipment at factory shop prices in all age ranges.
There is also a shoe museum, children's playground (indoor
and outdoor), picnic area and cafe. Admission free, and there is
a pay and display car park.

When washing a baby's or small child's hair, smear a little petroleum jelly
above the eyebrows and this will stop water or suds running into the eyes
as it should direct the suds to the side of the face.

CRAZY MAC'S

FLEET LANE, FLEETBRIDGE, POOLE, DORSET BH15 3BZ
☎ (01202) 666567. OPEN SEVEN DAYS A WEEK.
Enormous 62,000 sq ft outlet selling liquidated, salvage and
clearance stock from furniture to electrical goods. There is a
children's clothing department and the outlet also sells toys,
bunk beds, cots, prams and, depending on what comes in, a
variety of other child-oriented merchandise.

CROCKERS

2 EASTOVER, BRIDGWATER, SOMERSET TA6 5AB
☎ (01278) 452617. OPEN 9 – 5.30 MON – SAT, 11 – 5
SUN.
10A HIGH STREET, BURNHAM-ON-SEA,
SOMERSET TA8 1NX
☎ (01278) 794668. OPEN 9 – 5.30 MON – SAT, 11 – 5
SUN, 10 – 5 BANK HOLIDAYS.
112-114 HIGH STREET, STREET, SOMERSET BA16 0EW
☎ (01458) 42055. OPEN 9 – 5.30 MON – SAT, 11 – 5 SUN,
10 – 5 BANK HOLIDAYS.
THE FACTORY SHOP, CLARKS VILLAGE, STREET,
SOMERSET BA16 0YA
☎ (01458) 43131. OPEN 9 – 6 MON – SAT, 11 – 5 SUN,
9 – 6 BANK HOLIDAYS.
UNIT G13, WEST SWINDON DISTRICT CENTRE, SWINDON,
WILTSHIRE SN5 7DI
☎ (01793) 873662. OPEN 9 – 8 MON   FRI, 9 – 6 SAT,
10 – 4 SUN, 10 – 5 BANK HOLIDAYS.
UNIT 2, WORLE SHOPPING CENTRE, WORLE,
AVON BS22 0BT
☎ (01934) 521693. OPEN 9 – 8 MON – FRI, 9 – 6 SAT,
11 – 5 SUN, 9 – 5 BANK HOLIDAYS.
Clarks International operate a chain of factory shops nationally
which specialise in selling slight seconds and ends of lines from
Clarks Shoes, K Shoes and other brands for children. These
trade under the name of Crockers, K Factory shop or Clarks
Factory Shop and while not all are physically attached to a shoe

factory, these shops are treated as factory shops by the company. Customers can expect to find a wide choice of children's shoes, from Clarks, K Shoes, Dr Martens and famous name brands in trainers, although all are not sold in every outlet. Discounts are on average around 30% off the normal high street price for perfect stock.

GEMMA

422 LYMINGTON ROAD, HIGHCLIFFE, CHRISTCHURCH, DORSET BH23 5RR
☎ (01425) 276928. OPEN 10 – 5 MON – SAT, 10 – 1 WED.
Women's nearly-new shop which also stocks childrenswear up to the age of seven, plus there is a separate play area for children.

KARALYNE'S

20 WEST STREET, WILTON, WILTSHIRE
☎ (01722) 742802. OPEN 9.30 – 4, MON – SAT, CLOSED WED.
Tiny but full shop selling nearly-new clothing and accessories for women and children at bargain prices, including maternity wear. Stocks more than 1,000 items at a time with a constant flow of new arrivals, most of which are aimed at women but there is a reasonable selection of childrenswear for all ages and sometimes even school uniforms. Children's play corner.

KENT & CAREY

THE STUDIO, DAIRY HOUSE FARM, ALLINGTON, CHIPPENHAM, WILTSHIRE SN14 6LJ
☎ (1249) 656926. PHONE FIRST.
Makers of traditional nightwear for children – navy striped long pyjamas with ships trim, sailor teddies rompers – Kent & Carey has recently added swimwear and casual clothes to its range. Designs include blue daisy, floral rosebud, turquoise teacups, blue gingham, blue sheep, sailor teddies and turquoise floral. They also still produce the Sleepcozy with which they began the business, now available in Beatrix Potter and other designs

and approved by The Cot Death Society. With twice-yearly collections, there are always bargains to be had in terms of end of season lines, samples, etc, at reductions of up to 30%.

KIDS' STUFF
10 HENSMANS HILL, CLIFTON, BRISTOL, AVON BS8 4PE
☎ (0117) 9734980. OPEN 9 – 5 MON – FRI, 9.30 – 5.30 SAT.

In operation for more than 16 years, Kids' Stuff sells high quality children's clothes (no coats or underwear), most of which are in 100% cotton or wool, for babies to 12-year-olds. Sited under the factory where the clothes are made, the factory shop sells over-runs, discontinued lines and ex-catalogue items at up to 50% discount, though most of the stock is new, perfect and at full price.

MATALAN
UNIT 2, HAVEN BANKS, WATER LANE, EXETER,
DEVON EX2 8DW
☎ (01392) 413375. OPEN 10 – 8 MON – FRI, 9 – 6 SAT,
11 – 5 SUN.
UNIT 1, ALDERMOOR WAY, LONGWELL GREEN,
BRISTOL BS15 7DA
☎ (0117) 9352828. OPEN 10 – 8 MON – FRI, 9 – 6 SAT,
11 – 5 SUN.
UNITS 2 & 3, TURBARY RETAIL PARK, RINGWOOD ROAD,
POOLE, DORSET BH12 3JJ
☎ (01202) 590686. OPEN 10 – 8 MON – FRI, 9 – 6 SAT,
11 – 5 SUN.

A former cash and carry company, Matalan has now become a discount club operation which sells 90% clothing and 10% household items, toiletries and luggage. Members are usually employees whose company is registered with Matalan, senior citizens with a pension through one of the listed companies, or anyone who is VAT-registered. But members of the public can gain access with a day pass. Merchandise is sold at between 20%–50% cheaper than high street prices. And unlike many discount club operations, you don't have to buy in bulk. There's a wide range of children's clothing including jeans, denim jackets, coats, girls' dresses, jumpers and jogging suits, with more merchandise for babies and children under 9, although the age range does go up to about 12.

MILL SHOP

KING STREET, WILTON, SALISBURY, WILTSHIRE SP2 0AY
☎ (01722) 744183. OPEN 9 – 5 MON – SAT, 11 – 5 SUN.
The Mill Shop above the Royal Wilton Carpet Factory sells a variety of clothing, including children's, all of which are factory seconds. Stock for children varies but has included babygros to sweatshirts, boys' trousers to rugby shirts, dresses to tracksuit bottoms. Many have had the labels removed.

MORLANDS FACTORY SHOP

A39 BETWEEN GLASTONBURY AND STREET, SOMERSET
☎ (01458) 835042. OPEN 9.30 – 5 MON – SAT.
Morlands sheepskin has been manufactured here for more than 120 years. Most of the stock is for adults, but there are children's sheepskin coats, suede and leather jackets, sheepskin slippers, mittens and hats for ages two to fourteen.

ROUNDABOUT

2 PRIOR PARK ROAD, WIDCOMBE, BATH, AVON BA2 4NG
☎ (01225) 316696. OPEN 9.30 – 5 MON – SAT.
Nearly-new and new samples of childrenswear from birth to the age of twelve from Cakewalk and Mothercare to Oilily and Naf Naf at discounts of about 40%–50% for brand new samples. Nearly-new clothes range from £2 for a babygro and include footwear and toys. Also great savings on secondhand cots, playpens, prams, car seats and baby alarms. Limited parking near the shop, but there is a car park across the road.

SCHOOL GEAR SERVICE

1B BATH PLACE, TAUNTON, SOMERSET TA1
☎ (01823) 284031. OPEN 10 – 5 TUES, WED, OR PHONE
FOR AN APPOINTMENT.

Operates from a tiny room above a double glazing shop and sells secondhand school uniforms and equipment as well as some children's "mufti". Mrs Evemy has been running the business for twelve years and also sells football and rugby boots from £4.50, riding hats, ballet outfits, tap shoes, hockey sticks starting at £4.59 and cricket bats as well as local public and state school uniforms.

THE FACTORY SHOP

36-37 ROUNDSTONE STREET, TROWBRIDGE, WILTSHIRE
BA14 8DE
☎ (01225) 751399. OPEN 9 – 5.30 MON – SAT.
MART ROAD, MINEHEAD, SOMERSET TA24 5BJ
☎ (01643) 705911. OPEN 9.30 – 5.30 SEVEN DAYS A
WEEK AND BANK HOLIDAYS IN SUMMER, 9.30 – 5.30
MON – SAT, 11 – 5 SUN IN WINTER.

The Factory Shop carries a constantly changing variety of infants' and children's clothing, footwear and accessories, specialising in chainstore and branded ends of lines and slight seconds. All the major store brands are carried from time to time, with the age range covering birth to twelve years. New deliveries are made weekly and in some cases daily, so it is impossible to say what is in each store at any one time. All merchandise is on sale at around one-third off the high street prices, but customers have to be quick to get the best bargains. Babywear is just one department – stores also stock Footwear, Clothing, Household Goods, Toiletries and Bedding.

If you're pregnant, don't forget that you are eligible for free dental treatment and prescriptions up to one year after the birth of your baby. You'll also be given free booklets on parenthood by your health visitor or ante natal clinic.

THE SHOE SHED

C/O NORMANS LTD, STATION ROAD, BUDLEIGH
SALTERTON, DEVON EX9 6RU
☎ (01395) 443399. OPEN 8.30 – 5.30 MON – WED,
8.30 – 8 THURS, FRI, 8.30 – 5.30 SAT, 10 – 4 SUN.
C/O NORMANS LTD, 23 FAIRMILE ROAD, CHRISTCHURCH,
DORSET BH23 2LA
☎ (01202) 474123. OPEN 10 – 6 TUES – THUR, 10 – 7 FRI,
9.30 – 5.30 SAT, 10 – 4 SUN.
C/O NORMANS LTD, MANDEVILLE ROAD, WYKE REGIS,
WEYMOUTH, DORSET DT4 9HW
☎ (01305) 766772. OPEN 8.30 – 5.30 MON – FRI,
8.30 – 5.30 SAT, 10 – 4 SUN.
Wide range of quality footwear at below retail prices. There are
no seconds – just perfects, as you would expect from a high
street store. They stock a variety of brand names such as Dunlop
and for very young babies trying their first shoes, Dandystepps.
Sizes start from 2 and prices from £4.50. They also stock their
own quality shoes, The Jennings Collection – prices start from
£7.50 – and their Reflex range of sports shoes. Staff are friendly
and willing to help.

TRAGO MILL

REGIONAL SHOPPING CENTRE, NEWTON ABBOT TQ12 6JD
☎ (01626) 821111. OPEN 9 – 5.30 MON – SAT.
2 WATERSFOOT, LISKEARD, CORNWALL
☎ (01579) 20584. OPEN 9 – 5.30 MON – SAT.
ARWANAKS STREET, FALMOUTH TR11 3LF
☎ (01326) 315738. OPEN 9 – 5.30 MON – SAT,
10.15 – 4.55 SUN
Children's clothes and footwear from underwear to coats at
competitive prices. Stock varies, but there is sometimes Marks
& Spencer outfits and Lee Cooper jeans. In the bedding
department, you can sometimes find cot quilts and children's
bedding.

WALES AND WEST MIDLANDS

BAIRDWEAR RACKE

108c Harcourt, Halesfield 13, Telford, Shropshire
☎ (01952) 684524. Open 9 – 4.30 Mon – Thur, 9 – 1 Fri.
Small selection of children's clothes, mostly for the under fives,
as the rest of the outlet is devoted to menswear.

BUMPSADAISY

25 Friars Street, Worcester
☎ (0905) 28993. Phone For Opening Times.
Franchised hire shops with large range of special occasion
maternity wear, from wedding outfits to ball gowns, to hire and
to buy. Hire costs average about £30 for special occasion wear.
Phone 0171-379 9831 for details of your local stockist.

BURBERRY

Ynyswen Road, Treorchy, Rhondda, Mid Glamorgan,
Wales
☎ (01443) 772020. Open 9 – 4 Mon – Thur, 9 – 2 Fri,
9 – 1.30 Sat.
Most of the Burberry factory shops sell seconds and overmakes
of the famous name raincoats and duffle coats, as well as
accessories such as the distinctive umbrellas, scarves and
handbags, plus gift food items. All carry the Burberry label and
are about one third of the normal retail price. Childrenswear
tends to be thin on the ground, so phone before visiting.

An American tip for clean sheets when trying to leave the nappy off your
toddler overnight: make a sheet sandwich of a rubber sheet, a dry sheet, a
rubber sheet, a dry sheet. When he or she wets the bed, just strip off the
top set of wet sheet and rubber sheet, revealing the bottom dry set.

CHARNOS

THE OLD SCHOOL BUILDING, OUTCLOUGH ROAD, BRINDLEY
FORD, STOKE-ON-TRENT, STAFFORDSHIRE
☎ (0782) 523485.
Ends of lines of baby clothes, babygros, vests, socks, bibs, plus
bedding and towelling at factory shop prices.

IMPS

69B HIGH STREET, WITNEY, OXFORDSHIRE
☎ (01993) 779875. OPEN 9 – 5 MON – SAT.
40 UPPER HIGH STREET, THAME, OXFORDSHIRE
☎ (01844) 212985. OPEN 9 – 5 MON – SAT.
52 SHEEP STREET, BICESTER, OXFORDSHIRE
☎ (01869) 243455. OPEN 9 – 5 MON – SAT.
26 MARKET PLACE, HENLEY-ON-THAMES, OXFORDSHIRE
☎ (01491) 411530. OPEN 9 – 5 MON – SAT.
High street shop selling quality chainstore seconds for all the
family. Baby and childrenswear include vest and knickers 99p
each, socks 75p, jeans £6.99, pyjamas £11.99, smocked dresses
£8.99, denim shirts for ages 2/3 £5, taffeta party dresses for ages
5/6 £10, velvet party dresses for ages 2/3 £6, long jumpers
£6.99, Mickey Mouse tracksuits for ages 7/8 £11.99, floral girl's
trousers for age 8 £8.99. Stock changes constantly.

JEN SHOES

CASTLEFIELDS, NEWPORT ROAD, STAFFORD, WEST
MIDLANDS ST16 1BQ
☎ (0785) 211311. OPEN 10 – 4 SEVEN DAYS A WEEK.
Has thousands of pairs of shoes from fashion footwear and
sandals to slippers, sports shoes, boots and children's shoes in
its factory shop, ranging from children's size 6.

If you have to remove a splinter from a child's finger, it is a good idea to
rub the spot with an ice cube first. The cold will act as an anaesthetic and
reduce the pain.

LILLIPUT AND JACK IN THE BOX

63 Avon Crescent, Stratford-upon-Avon,
Warwickshire
☎ (01789) 267991. Open 10 – 4 Tue – Sat.
Children's toys, secondhand clothes and baby equipment from
0–10 years.

LITTLE GEMS

20 Coten End, Warwickshire CV34 4NP
☎ (01926) 408248. Open 10 – 5 Mon – Fri, 10.30 – 4
Sat.
Nearly-new clothes and equipment for babies to 12 year olds.
Labels include Oilily, Jean le Bourget, Chicaloo, Laura Ashley
and Start Smart. Equipment ranges from high chairs and
playpens to prams, buggies and Moses baskets, usually at less
than half the normal retail price. There are also secondhand
toys from Fisher-Price to Matchbox, as well as sterilisers, breast
pumps, stair gates, fire guards, cots, sleeping bags, bed linen
and cot linen, matinee jackets and shawls. At time of going to
press, they were planning to offer a hire service, too.

M C HITCHEN & SONS LTD

299 Coventry Road, Birmingham,
West Midlands B10 0RA
☎ (0121) 772 1637. Open 9 – 5.30 Mon – Sat.
236 Hawthorn Road, Kingstanding,
Birmingham B44 8PP
☎ (0121) 373 1276. Open 9.15 – 5.30 Mon – Sat.
Littlewoods mail order catalogue sale shops, most of which are
in the north of England, offer up to 40% off the catalogue price
of clothing and between 50% and 60% off electrical goods.
They also run a mobile shop which operates in cities where they
don't have a sale shop. For details for future venues for the
mobile sales, which usually take place once a month, contact
Mrs Jean Banks, c/o Crosby DC, Kershaw Avenue, Endbutt
Lane, Crosby, Merseyside L70 1AH; (0151) 928 6611.

MAJOR SAVINGS

38 City Arcade, Coventry, West Midlands CV1 3HW
☎ (01203) 553355. Open 9 – 5.30 Mon – Sat.
Formerly a Manorgrove shop, selling ex-catalogue lines from
Grattan, Major Savings now also sells Scoops catalogue
overstocks as well as Grattan. These consist mainly of clothes
for all the family, but there is usually a selection for babies and
children, as well as some bedding and nursery equipment.
Stock depends on what is returned, unsold or has damaged
packaging.

MATALAN

Unit 5, The John Allen Centre, Cowley, Oxford,
Oxfordshire OX4 3JP
☎ (01865) 747400. Open 10 – 8 Mon – Fri, 9 – 6 Sat,
11 – 5 Sun.
Unit A1/A2, Gallagher Retail Park, Tewkesbury
Road, Cheltenham, Gloucestershire GL51 9RR
☎ (01242) 254001. Open 10 – 8 Mon – Fri, 9 – 6 Sat,
11 – 5 Sun.
Unit 1, Meole Brace Retail Park, Hereford Road,
Shrewsbury SY3 9NB
☎ (01743) 363240. Open 10 – 8 Mon – Fri, 9 – 6 Sat,
11 – 5 Sun.
Unit 7, Ventura Shopping Centre, Ventura Park
Road, Tamworth, Staffordshire B78 3HB
☎ (01827) 50900. Open 10 – 8 Mon – Fri, 9 – 6 Sat,
11 – 5 Sun.
Foundry Road, Morriston, Swansea SA6 8DU
☎ (01792) 792229. Open 10 – 8 Mon – Fri, 9 – 6 Sat,
11 – 5 Sun.
Birmingham Road, Howard Street, Wolverhampton,
West Midlands WV2 2LQ
☎ (01902) 352813. Open 10 – 8 Mon – Fri, 9 – 6 Sat,
11 – 5 Sun.

UNIT 4B, CWMBRAN RETAIL PARK, CWNBRAN DRIVE,
CWNBRAN, GWENT NP44 3JQ
☎ (01633) 866944. OPEN 10 – 8 MON – FRI, 9 – 6 SAT,
11 – 5 SUN.

UNIT E, MAYBIRD CENTRE, BIRMINGHAM ROAD,
STRATFORD-UPON-AVON CV37 0HZ
☎ (01789) 262223. OPEN 10 – 8 MON – FRI, 9 – 6 SAT,
11 – 5 SUN.

UNIT 1A & 1B, CAENARFON ROAD, BANGOR LL57 4SU.
☎ (01248) 362778. OPEN 10 – 8 MON – FRI, 9 – 6 SAT,
11 – 5 SUN.

WOLSTANTON RETAIL PARK, WOLSTANTON, NEWCASTLE,
STAFFORDSHIRE ST5 1DY
☎ (01782) 711731. OPEN 9.30 – 8 MON – FRI, 9 – 6 SAT,
11 – 5 SUN.

UNITS 5 & 6, QUEENSVILLE RETAIL PARK, SILKMORE LANE,
STAFFORD ST17 4SU
☎ (01785) 226211. OPEN 10 – 8 MON – FRI, 9 – 6 SAT,
11 – 5 SUN.

UNIT 2, 282-284 NEWPORT ROAD, CARDIFF CF3 7AE
☎ (01222) 491781. OPEN 10 – 8 MON – FRI, 9 – 6 SAT,
11 – 5 SUN.

UNIT A, LICHFIELD STREET, BURTON ON TRENT,
STAFFORDSHIRE DE14 3QZ
☎ (01283) 540856. OPEN 10 – 8 MON – FRI, 9 – 6 SAT,
11 – 5 SUN.

A former cash and carry company, Matalan has now become a
discount club operation which sells 90% clothing and 10%
household items, toiletries and luggage at its 37 branches
countrywide. Members are usually employees whose company
is registered with Matalan, senior citizens with a pension
through one of the listed companies, or anyone who is VAT-
registered. But members of the public can gain access on a
Thursday with a day pass. Merchandise is sold at between
20%–50% cheaper than high street prices. And unlike many
discount club operations, you don't have to buy in bulk. There's
a wide range of children's clothing, including jeans, denim

jackets, coats, girls' dresses, jumpers and jogging suits, with more merchandise for babies and children under 9, although the age range does go up to about 12.

PIERETTE LTD

LUTTERWORTH ROAD, BURBAGE, HINCKLEY, LEICESTERSHIRE LE10 2DJ

☎ (01455) 633703. OPEN 9 – 5 MON – FRI, 9 – 4.30 SAT, 10 – 4.30 SUN.

Chainstore seconds for all the family, including a complete range of childrenswear from birth to teens. Also children's novelty gifts such as Red Riding Hood dolls, and slippers but no other footwear.

ROSS LABELS LTD

OVERROSS HOUSE, ROSS-ON-WYE, HEREFORDSHIRE HR9 7QJ

☎ (01989) 769000. OPEN 10 – 6 MON, 10 – 6 TUE, WED, SUN, 10 – 7 THUR, 10 – 5 FRI, 9 – 6 SAT.

Warehouse measuring 22,000 square feet and selling a wide range of quality clothes at reduced prices, many with discounts of 20%–50%. They have a large childrenswear department with clothes for babies to older children – dresses, jeans including Lee Cooper, jogging suits, coats, rainwear, socks – but no footwear. Easy and free parking, disabled facilities, cafeteria.

SECOND TIME AROUND

13B PARK STREET, LEAMINGTON SPA, WARWICKSHIRE CV32 4QN

☎ (01926) 889811. OPEN 10 – 5 TUE – SAT.

Nearly-new children's clothes from babies to teenagers which covers a wide spectrum of labels from Marks & Spencer and Mothercare to OshKosh and Oilily. The shop caters mostly for women, but has a good selection of children's clothes.

SECONDS OUT

6 GREAT DARKGATE STREET, ABERYSTWYTH, DYFED
☎ (01970) 611897. OPEN 9.30 – 5.30 MON – SAT.
Makes trousers for high street department stores, overmakes
and seconds of which are sold in the factory shop. The trousers
are for children and adults. Children's sizes range from age two
to sixteen. There are jeans, school trousers, mini Chinos, casual
trousers, jodphurs but no leggings. Prices range from £8–£15.

STEWART SECONDS

12 PIER STREET, ABERYSTWYTH, DYFED, WALES
☎ (01970) 611437. OPEN 9 – 5.30 MON – SAT, 11 – 5
SUN IN SUMMER.
14 NOTT SQUARE, CARMARTHEN, DYFED, WALES
☎ (01297) 222294. OPEN 9 – 5.30 MON – SAT.
HARFORD SQUARE, LAMPETER, DYFED, WALES
☎ (01570) 422205. OPEN 9.30 – 5.30 MON – SAT.
Y MAES, PWLLHELI, GWYNEDD, NORTH WALES
☎ (01758) 701130. OPEN 9 – 5.30 MON – SAT.
Branded merchandise from most of the major UK chain stores,
all well-known high street department store names at half the
retail store price. Clothes range from babywear to young
teenage outfits, and there is also bedding for babies and for
older children, towels and some soft toys. The Gwynedd branch
does not stock a lot of bedding for children.

THE FACTORY SHOP

NEWLAND, WITNEY, OXFORDSHIRE
☎ (01993) 708338. OPEN 10 – 5 MON – SAT.
Part of the Coats Viyella group, which makes clothes for high
street department stores, this medium-sized factory shop caters
for all the family. Children's items make up about 20% of the
stock, but that can vary. When we were there, we saw vests and
knickers 99p each, school sweaters £3.99, denim dresses for
ages 10–11 £9.99, boys' waistcoats £9.99, hat and scarf sets
£1.99, and a mixture of shorts, leggings and summer dresses for
about £6.99.

THE FACTORY SHOP
NEW ROAD, PERSHORE, WORCESTERSHIRE WR10 1BT
☎ (01386) 556467. OPEN 9 – 5 MON – SAT, 10.30 – 4.30
SUN AND BANK HOLIDAYS.
Sells everything from babywear to outfits for older children up
to the age of nine, including tracksuits, swimwear, underwear,
dresses, trousers, coats, rainwear, slippers, wellingtons, and
some toys, baby's bottles, changing bags, baby oil and baby
toiletries. There is some children's bedding, including the
occasional cot blanket. Most stock is seconds or clearance lines
from well-known chain stores and department stores such as
Marks & Spencer, Adams and Mothercare.

THE FACTORY SHOP
WESTWARD ROAD, COUNTY RETAIL PARK, CAINSCROSS,
STROUD, GLOUCESTERSHIRE GL5 4JE
☎ (01453) 756655. OPEN 9 – 5 MON – THUR, SAT, 9 – 6
FRI, 10 – 4 SUN AND BANK HOLIDAYS.
NEW ROAD, PERSHORE, WORCESTERSHIRE WR10 1BY
☎ (01386) 556467. OPEN 9 – 5 MON – SAT, 10.30 – 4.30
SUN AND BANK HOLIDAYS.
THE FASHION WEARHOUSE, CORPORATION STREET, RUGBY,
WARWICKSHIRE CV21 2DN
☎ (01788) 542253. OPEN 10 – 6 MON – SAT, 11 – 5 SUN.
The Factory Shop carries a constantly changing variety of
infants' and children's clothing, footwear and accessories,
specialising in chainstore and branded ends of lines and slight
seconds. All the major store brands are carried from time to
time, with the age range covering birth to 12 years. New
deliveries are made weekly and in some cases daily, so it is
impossible to say what is in each store at any one time. All
merchandise is on sale at around one-third off the high street
prices, but customers have to be quick to get the best bargains.
Babywear is just one department – stores also stock Footwear,
Clothing, Household Goods, Toiletries and Bedding.

THE SHOE SHED

CASTLEFIELDS, NEWPORT ROAD, STAFFORD,
STAFFORDSHIRE ST16 1BQ
☎ (01785) 211311. OPEN 10 – 4 SEVEN DAYS A WEEK.
Wide range of quality footwear at below retail prices. There are
no seconds – just perfects, as you would expect from a high
street store. They stock a variety of brand names such as Pebe
and Dunlop and for very young babies trying their first shoes,
Dandystepps. Sizes start from 2 and prices from £4.50. They
also stock their own quality shoes, The Jennings Collection –
prices start from £7.50 – and their Reflex range of sports shoes.
Staff are friendly and willing to help. The shop is at the back of
the headquarters.

TOP MARKS

23 HIGH STREET, MORETON-IN-MARSH, GLOS GL56 0AF
☎ (01608) 651272. OPEN 9 – 5.30 MON – FRI, 9 – 5 SAT.
Leading chainstore quality seconds for all the family, although
there is usually less stock for children than for women and men.
The children's and babywear ranges are mostly Marks &
Spencer seconds, and there are no toys or baby equipment.

TREFIW WOOLLEN MILL SHOP

TREFIW, GWYNEDD LL27 0NQ
☎ (01492) 640462. OPEN 9 – 5 MON – FRI, 10 – 5 SAT.
Sells products manufactured on the premises: for children,
padded jackets from £27; fleece jackets, £22; waterproofs,
£10–£16; Arran jumpers and cardigans from £13–£20; sweatshirts, £8–£15. There is more stock for children in the summer
than in the winter.

TWEEDMILL FACTORY SHOP

LLANERCH PARK, ST ASAPH, CLWYD
☎ (01745) 730072. OPEN 10 – 6 SEVEN DAYS A WEEK.
Baby clothes and clothes for smaller children up to the age of
five: gloves, hats, mittens, shoes, jackets, all made by
manufacturers for high street stores but sold without the labels.

EAST ANGLIA AND EAST MIDLANDS

BALLY FACTORY SHOP

HALL ROAD, NORWICH, NORFOLK NR4 6DP
☎ (01603) 760590. OPEN 9.30 – 5.30 MON – FRI, 9 – 5.30 SAT, 10 – 4 BANK HOLIDAYS.
The Bally factory shop is situated next to the main factory and its range includes children's footwear, from slippers, sandals and shoes to boots and wellingtons, sizes 3–12. Prices for shoes start at about £6.99 – which usually represents half the normal shop price – for merchandise which is rejects, substandard, and ends of line of ex-sale stock. Stock changes constantly and there is a coffee shop, children's play area, free parking and disabled facilities.

BARRATT'S SHOES

BARRACK ROAD, KINGSTHORPE HOLLOW, NORTHAMPTON, NORTHAMPTONSHIRE
☎ (01604) 718632. OPEN 9 – 5.30 MON – SAT.
Reject trainers and ex-window display shoes at factory prices among a range of perfect shoes from sizes 4 upwards, the latter of which are sold at sale prices.

BLUNTS

128-132 GRAMBY STREET, LEICESTER LE1 1DL
☎ (0116) 2555959. OPEN 8.30 – 6 MON – SAT 10 – 4 SUN, 10 – 5 BANK HOLIDAYS.
Children's sale shoes range from £4.99 and from size 3 upwards.

BYFORD HOSIERY

ABBEY LANE, LEICESTER, LEICESTERSHIRE

☎ (01533) 611135. OPEN 9.30 – 5 MON – SAT.

Children's clothes which are chainstore seconds at half the price to fit babies from twelve months to teenagers, though the babywear range isn't large. Plenty of underwear, night clothes, dresses, socks, trousers, leisure wear, shirts and knitwear.

CASTAWAYS

10 BURTON ROAD, LINCOLN LN1 3LB

☎ (01522) 546035. OPEN 9.30 – 4.30 MON – SAT, CLOSED WEDS.

An agency shop specialising in almost new children's clothing, nursery equipment, toys and ladies' fashions and accessories. Smart mums-to-be know this is the place to go to find not only a complete wardrobe but also the layette. Only items that look virtually new and are fashionable are selected for sale.

CHARNOS

AMBER BUSINESS CENTRE, GREENHILL LANE, RIDDINGS, DERBYSHIRE

☎ (01773) 540408. OPEN 10 – 5 TUE – FRI, 9.30 – 1 SAT.

CORPORATION ROAD, ILKESTON, DERBYSHIRE

☎ (0115) 9440301. OPEN 2 – 5 TUE – FRI, 9.30 – 1 SAT.

Ends of lines of baby clothes, babygros, vests, socks, bibs, plus bedding and towelling at factory shop prices.

COURTAULDS CHILDRENSWEAR

NIX HILL, ALFRETON, DERBYSHIRE DE55 7FQ

☎ (01773) 833421. OPEN 9 – 5 MON – SAT.

Clothes for boys and girls from birth to twelve years, including tights, underwear from £1.25, cord trousers, knitwear, coats, thermal socks from 99p to £1.25, sweatshirts from £9.99, and shirts from £6.99.

COURTAULDS LEISUREWEAR

HIGH STREET, HEANOR, DERBYSHIRE
☎ (01773) 530206. OPEN 9 – 3.50 MON, TUE, THUR, FRI,
10 – 3 SAT.
Chainstore seconds or overmakes of children's clothes ages
three to twelve. Underwear and outerwear, tracksuits and
occasional babywear at one third off the normal retail prices.

COURTAULDS MERIDIAN

HAYDN ROAD, NOTTINGHAM, NOTTINGHAMSHIRE
MG5 1DH
☎ (0115) 9246100. OPEN 9 – 5 MON – FRI, 9 – 5.30 SAT.
Large range of children's clothes from 12 months to about seven
or eight years. Underwear, socks, knitwear, jeans, trousers,
skirts, dresses, leisurewear, coats for boys and girls. Plus Zorbit
baby range for the nursery: cot quilts, pram quilts, duvets,
curtains and lamp shades. Also some children's bedding with
Peter Pan and Mr Blobby designs. There is a coffee shop on site
and a car park.

COURTAULDS TEXTILES

ELLIS STREET, KIRKBY IN ASHFIELD, NOTTINGHAMSHIRE
NG17 7AL
☎ (01623) 754193. OPEN 9 – 5 MON – SAT.
Range of clothes from underwear to coats made by Courtaulds
for Marks & Spencer, Adams, Mothercare and other brands – all
without their labels – to fit children from infancy to teenage
years. There is also a Shoe Shed within the factory complex
where a full range of shoes at factory shop prices can be bought.

COURTAULDS TEXTILES

ALLENBY INDUSTRIAL ESTATE, CROFTON CLOSE, LINCOLN,
LINCOLNSHIRE LN2 5QT
☎ (01522) 539859. OPEN 9 – 5 MON – SAT.
Chainstore seconds and ends of lines for children at discounts of
at least 20%.

CROCKERS

111 Front Street, Arnold, Nottinghamshire
NG5 7ED
☎ (0115) 9674212. Open 9 – Mon – Sat, 10 – 4 Sun
and Bank Holidays.

Clarks International operate a chain of factory shops nationally
which specialise in selling slight seconds and ends of lines from
Clarks Shoes, K Shoes and other brands for children. These
trade under the name of Crockers, K Factory shop or Clarks
Factory Shop and while not all are physically attached to a shoe
factory, these shops are treated as factory shops by the
company. Customers can expect to find a wide choice of
children's shoes, from Clarks, K Shoes, Dr Martens and famous
name brands in trainers, although all are not sold in every
outlet. Discounts are on average around 30% off the normal
high street price for perfect stock.

DINDY'S

Hawstead House, Hawstead, Bury St Edmunds,
Suffolk IP29 5NL
☎ (01284) 388276. Open 10 – 4 Tue & Thur, 10 – 1 Sat.
Closed During State School Holidays.

Set in a converted stables, Dindy's sells high quality second
hand clothes for women with a small selection of childrenswear
from three years up to teenagers.

GEORGE BRETTLES FACTORY SHOP

Chapel Street, Belper, Derbyshire
☎ (01773) 821532. Open 9 – 4 Mon – Fri, 9 – 2.30 Sat.

Babies' and childrenswear up to the age of five including
babygros, jumpers, skirts, and occasionally pyjamas up to the
age of twelve. Most are chainstore makes.

When on holiday, tie a coloured balloon to your deck chair. The children
will be able to spot you on a crowded beach, saving tears and worry.

GLAD RAGS

24 HIGH STREET, HADLEIGH, IPSWICH, SUFFOLK
☎ (01473) 827768. OPEN 9.30 – 4 TUE, THUR – SAT.
Range of nearly-new outfits for women and children, although
childrenswear, both English and Continental for 0–10 year olds,
is sold very quickly.

GLOVERALL

LONDON ROAD, WELLINGBOROUGH, NORTHAMPTONSHIRE
NN8 2QH
☎ (01933) 225183. OPEN 10 – 5 TUE – FRI, 10 – 4.30 SAT.
The award-winning duffle coat manufacturer has a factory shop
selling woollen mix duffle coats at half the normal retail price.
Children's duffle coats start at £20 and there are usually at least
20 in stock in each size, but phone before you make a journey as
colour availability may not suit.

M C HITCHEN & SONS LTD

7 HIGH STREET, GRANTHAM, LINCOLNSHIRE NG31 6PN
☎ (01476) 590552. OPEN 9.30 – 5.30 MON, 9 – 5.30
TUE – SAT.
Littlewoods mail order catalogue sale shops, most of which are
in the north of England, offer up to 40% off the catalogue price
of clothing and between 50% and 60% off electrical goods.
They also run a mobile shop which operates in cities where they
don't have a sale shop. For details for future venues for the
mobile sales, which usually take place once a month, contact
Mrs Jean Banks, c/o Crosby DC, Kershaw Avenue, Endbutt
Lane, Crosby, Merseyside L70 1AH; (0151) 928 6611.

MAGPIE

BRIDGE STREET, ST IVES, HUNTINGDON, CAMBRIDGESHIRE
☎ (01480) 461808.
Nearly-new clothes for children.

MATALAN

UNIT 1, WEEDON ROAD INDUSTRIAL ESTATE, TYNE ROAD, NORTHAMPTON NN5 5BE
☎ (01604) 589119. OPEN 10 – 8 MON – FRI, 9 – 6 SAT, 11 – 5 SUN.

UNIT 1, PHOENIX RETAIL CENTRE, PHOENIX PARKWAY, CORBY NN17 5DT
☎ (01536) 408042. OPEN 10 – 8 MON – FRI, 9 – 6 SAT, 11 – 5 SUN.

BLACKFRIARS ROAD, KINGS LYNN, NORFOLK PE30 1RX
☎ (01553) 765696. OPEN 10 – 8 MON – FRI, 9 – 6 SAT, 11 – 5 SUN.

EAST STATION ROAD, PETERBOROUGH, CAMBRIDGESHIRE PE2 8AA
☎ (01733) 341229. OPEN 10 – 8 MON – FRI, 9 – 6 SAT, 11 – 5 SUN.

LINDIS RETAIL PARK, TRITTON ROAD, LINCOLN
☎ (01522) 696541. OPEN 10 – 8 MON – FRI, 9 – 6 SAT, 11 – 5 SUN.

A former cash and carry company, Matalan has now become a discount club operation which sells 90% clothing and 10% household items, toiletries and luggage at its 37 branches countrywide. Members are usually employees whose company is registered with Matalan, senior citizens with a pension through one of the listed companies, or anyone who is VAT-registered. But members of the public can gain access on a Thursday with a day pass. Merchandise is sold at between 20%–50% cheaper than high street prices. And unlike many discount club operations, you don't have to buy in bulk. There's a wide range of children's clothing, including jeans, denim jackets, coats, girls' dresses, jumpers and jogging suits, with more merchandise for babies and children under 9, although the age range does go up to about 12.

ORCHIDS
3 PARK STREET, TOWCESTER, NORTHAMPTONSHIRE
NN12 6DQ
☎ (01327) 358455. OPEN 9.30 – 5 MON – SAT.
Nearly-new children's clothes from birth to twelve years. There
are usually at least three rails of clothes ranging from Marks &
Spencer, Mothercare and Laura Ashley to OshKosh, Oilily and
Gap, plus a rail of snowsuits and coats – in season. There is
usually a greater selection of girls' outfits than boys'.

SHEERS LTD
ST MARY'S STREET, EYNESBURY, ST NEOTS,
CAMBRIDGESHIRE
☎ (01480) 473476. OPEN 10 – 12 TUE, WED, 10 – 12 AND
2 – 3.30 THUR.
Babies' and toddlers' vests, babygros, all-in-ones, cot
quilts, towels, socks, underwear and T-shirts, most of which
are chainstore seconds and overmakes at discounts of up to
50%.

STAGE 2
SAVILLE ROAD, WESTWOOD, PETERBOROUGH,
CAMBRIDGESHIRE PE3 7PR
☎ (01733) 263308. OPEN 10 – 8 MON – FRI, 9 – 6 SAT
AND BANK HOLIDAYS.
THE RIVERSIDE RETAIL PARK, QUEEN'S DRIVE,
NOTTINGHAM NG2 1RU
☎ (015) 9865812. OPEN 10 – 8 MON – FRI, 9 – 6 SAT,
11 – 5 SUN AND BANK HOLIDAYS.
UNIT 3, TRITTON RETAIL PARK, CENTURION ROAD,
LINCOLN LN1
☎ (01522) 560303. OPEN 10 – 8 MON – FRI, 9 – 6 SAT,
10 – 4 BANK HOLIDAYS.
This is a Freeman's mail order discount store which sells the full
range of goods as seen in the catalogue at discount prices. There
are children's clothes from underwear to raincoats, toys, and
nursery equipment at 50% of the full catalogue price. There is

also a British shoe concession in the store, which also sells at discount.

START-RITE

DOMANI, 18 TOWER STREET, KING'S LYNN, NORFOLK
P30 1EJ
☎ (01553) 760786. OPEN 9 – 5.30 MON – SAT, 10 – 4
WED.
The children's shoe experts have a factory shop selling clearance lines of children's shoes from baby size two and a half upwards at discounts of one third, and seconds at discounts of fifty percent. They stock a full range of footwear; rejects are sold at half price; end of sales stock at discounts of one third.

THE FACTORY SHOP

SOUTH GREEN, EAST DEREHAM, NORFOLK NR19 1PR
☎ (01362) 691868. OPEN 9 – 5 MON – SAT, 10 – 4 SOME
BANK HOLIDAYS.
THE FACTORY SHOP, NEWBOLD FOOTWEAR, BROOK STREET,
SILEBY, LEICESTERSHIRE LE12 7RF
☎ (01509) 813514. OPEN 9 – 5 MON – SAT.
BARTON BUSINESS CENTRE, BARTON ROAD,
BURY ST EDMUNDS, SUFFOLK IP32 7BQ
☎ (01284) 701578. OPEN 9 – 5.30 MON – SAT, 11 – 5
SUN.
The Factory Shop carries a constantly changing variety of infants and children's clothing, footwear and accessories, specialising in chainstore and branded ends of lines and slight seconds. All the major store brands are carried from time to time, with the age range covering birth to twelve years. New deliveries are made weekly and in some cases daily, so it is impossible to say what is in each store at any one time. All merchandise is on sale at around one-third off the high street prices, but customers have to be quick to get the best bargains. Babywear is just one department – stores also stock Footwear, Clothing, Household Goods, Toiletries and Bedding.

THE UPPINGHAM DRESS AGENCY

2-6 ORANGE STREET, UPPINGHAM, RUTLAND LE15 9SQ
☎ (01572) 823276. OPEN 9 – 5.30 MON – SAT, 12 – 4
SUN AND BANK HOLIDAYS.

One of the oldest and possibly the largest dress agency in the country with 12 rooms on three floors packed with quality nearly-new clothing for children, men and women. One room on the first floor is devoted to children, although there are also children's sizes in the room with riding clothes and hacking jackets. Buggies can be left on the ground floor where there is a lounge with free coffee. Preference is given to designer labels, but better quality high street names are also stocked, so the children's ranges are anything from Marks & Spencer to Oilily and OshKosh and include quality footwear (Nike and Dr Martens). There are also new products such as waxed jackets and fleeced jackets at competitive prices. The proprietors are very selective about the condition of the merchandise and all stock is carefully vetted.

THE WORKSOP FACTORY SHOP

RAYMOTH LANE, WORKSOP, NOTTINGHAMSHIRE
☎ (01909) 472841. OPEN 9 – 5 MON – SAT, 11 – 5 SUN.

General babywear and children's clothes up to the age of nine or ten. Zorbit baby range of pretty bedding, cot quilts, and nursery accessories such as lampshades, plus coats, underwear, general clothes, mitts, helmets, towels, baby baskets, babygros. Mostly chainstore makes.

Fenland Aviation Museum features engines, uniforms, aeroplanes such as the Vampire T11 Jet Trainer, and Lightning Aircraft, parachutes and Thirties and Forties memorabilia. Entrance is only 50p for adults and 25p for children. It is situated in Bambers Garden Centre, where there is an aquatic centre and tea room and is open weekends and bank holidays only. Bambers Garden Centre is on Old Lynn Road, West Walton, Wisbech, Cambridgeshire. Phone 01945 585808.

VAGA FACTORY SHOP

BOWNE STREET, SUTTON IN ASHFIELD, NOTTINGHAM,
NOTTINGHAMSHIRE
☎ (01623) 442466. OPEN 9 – 4.30 MON – FRI, 9 – 3 SAT.
Sells seconds and discontinued lines of famous high street
brands including boys' schoolwear and leisure wear and
nightwear for girls aged 4–15.

WILLOW TRADING

WILLOWS TRADING ESTATE, FINBOROUGH ROAD,
STOWMARKET, SUFFOLK IP14 3BU
☎ (01499) 771261. OPEN 10 – 5.30 THUR – SAT.
A catalogue shop which sells catalogue returns from the
Freeman's mail order brochure. This can include anything the
catalogue sells, but stock varies so it is best to ring before
visiting. There are children's clothes from the Clothkits range,
as well as nursery equipment such as prams, pushchairs, and
cots.

Many women's magazines now have pages of freebies. For example, one
issue of *Practical Parenting* offered £4,000-worth of free gifts including 100
videos worth £9.99 each, and 50 bathtime kits worth £15 each. If you really
don't want to spend any money, nip into your local largest newsagent
where you won't be spotted noting down the details and then send in your
name and address and hope you strike lucky. The winners are usually
picked at random after a set closing date.

NORTH WEST, YORKSHIRE AND HUMBERSIDE

AS NEW FASHIONS

1 EMSCOTE GROVE, HAUGH SHAW ROAD, HALIFAX,
YORKSHIRE HX1 3AP
☎ (01422) 365379. OPEN 9.30 – 5 MON – SAT.
General nearly-new shop with a large section of children's clothes, including school uniforms, from babywear upwards. Skirts, trousers, shoes, slippers, trainers, many from Marks & Spencer, Adams, and some designer labels. Occasionally, they stock ballet outfits and sports wear, all at about one third of as-new prices.

BENETTON

HORNSEA FREEPORT SHOPPING VILLAGE, HORNSEA,
YORKSHIRE HU18 1UT
☎ (01964) 536791. OPEN 10 – 5 MON – FRI, 10 – 6 SAT,
SUN.
Benetton is just one of two dozen retailers which operate factory shops in this seaside spot in Yorkshire. The Benetton outlet looks just like a shop and sells previous season's stock as well as any returned merchandise and overmakes, and samples from Italy. Ages from birth to teens are catered for, but there are usually only small runs and stock varies. The Shopping Village has plenty to entertain the family with playgrounds, an indoor play centre, restaurants and butterfly world.

BURBERRY

WOODROW UNIVERSAL, JUNCTION MILLS, CROSS HILLS,
STEETON, NEAR KEIGHLEY, YORKSHIRE
☎ (01535) 633364. OPEN 1 – 5 MON – THUR, 2 – 5 FRI,
10 – 4 SAT.
Most of the Burberry factory shops sell seconds and overmakes of the famous name raincoats and duffle coats, as well as

accessories such as the distinctive umbrellas, scarves and handbags, plus gift food items. All carry the Burberry label and are about one third of the normal retail price. Childrenswear tends to be thin on the ground, so phone before visiting.

DALESOX

6 SWADFORD STREET, SKIPTON,
NORTH YORKSHIRE BD23 1JA
☎ (01756) 796509. OPEN 9 – 5 SEVEN DAYS A WEEK.
Based in Skipton's main shopping area, Dalesox sells quality hosiery and accessories. Most are perfect children's socks made for leading brand names and high street stores and cost about £1–£1.50 a pair, normal retail price up to £4.99. There is lots of design choice from Disney character socks to Wolsey Christmas pudding socks. There are also ski socks made for Lillywhites, pyjamas and nightshirts.

DAMART FACTORY CLEARANCE SHOP

UNIT 6A, ALSTON ROAD RETAIL PARK, BYPASS
ROUNDABOUT, BRADFORD ROAD, KEIGHLEY,
YORKSHIRE DD21 3NG
☎ (01535) 690648. OPEN 9 – 5 MON – SAT, 10 – 4 SUN
AND BANK HOLIDAYS.
Discontinued Damart fashion both outerwear and underwear for children of all ages, as well as gloves, shoes, hats and scarves.

ELITE DRESS AGENCY

1 MARKET STREET, ALTRINCHAM, CHESHIRE WA14 1QE
☎ (0161) 928 5424. OPEN 10 – 5 MON – SAT.
Good range of childrenswear in this ladies' dress agency including skirts, coats, trousers, sweaters dresses, but no sportswear or school uniforms. Age range is from eighteen months to about eleven.

EVERYTHING BUT THE BABY

19 KNARESBOROUGH ROAD, HARROGATE,
YORKSHIRE HG2 7SR
☎ (01423) 888292. OPEN 10 – 4 MON – SAT,
CLOSED 1 WED.

Nearly-new shop selling expansive range of babywear and baby equipment up to the age of five. Pushchairs and car seats, all fully checked, and clothes ranging from Marks & Spencer and Ladybird to OshKosh and Oilily.

FINSLEY MILL SHOP

FINSLEY GATE, BURNLEY, LANCASHIRE
☎ (01282) 425641. OPEN 9.30 – 5 MON – FRI, 9 – 4 SAT.

Children's shoes at discounts of up to 50% from toddlers' sizes upwards. Slippers, trainers, wellingtons, school and party shoes. There are also some clothes on sale here, but stock depends on availability.

FOSC DISCOUNT DEPARTMENT STORE

HULL ROAD, YORK, YORKSHIRE YO1 3JA
☎ (01904) 430481. OPEN 10 – 6 MON – SAT, 11 – 5 SUN.

Branded merchandise from more than 50 manufacturers which initially consisted of ends of lines, surplus stock, cancelled orders and slight seconds but is more likely now to be firsts. Some of the best-known high street names are here, at discounts of between 30%–70%. However, the labels are removed first. There is babywear, footwear, a limited range of toys and clothes for children from birth to twelve years. At time of going to press, there were plans to install baby changing facilities, film viewing and a play area. There is also a cafe, free car parking, disabled facilities and no membership is necessary.

Entertain your children in the car with cassette tapes of their favourite stories recorded by you. Or they can follow the words while listening to you – but don't forget to say "turn the page" when recording.

GOLDEN SHUTTLE MILL SHOP

ALBION ROAD, GREENGATES, BRADFORD BD10 9OQ
☎ (01274) 611161. OPEN 9.30 – 5 MON – SAT, MOST
BANK HOLIDAYS.
Children's clothes from 0–10 years. Babygros, cardigans, bibs, dresses, anoraks, mittens, socks, hats, sweaters, dresses from £6.99–£19.99, sleeping suits from £2.99, pyjamas and dressing gowns, but very little underwear. One section of the shop, which also caters for men and women, is devoted to babies and children. Joe Bloggs and Michael de Leon for boys is stocked.

GREAT CLOTHES

84 YORK ROAD, LEEDS, YORKSHIRE LS9 9AA
☎ (0113) 2350303. OPEN 9.30 – 9 MON – FRI, 9.30 – 6
SAT, 9.30 – 5 SUN.
Discounted clothes for children start at age 18 months; there are lots of items for girls and some for boys. Levi's, Wrangler and Pepe are stocked, but no underwear. Prices are about 25% cheaper than normal high street prices.

K SHOES

179-181 CENTRAL DRIVE, BLACKPOOL,
LANCASHIRE FY1 5ED
☎ (01253) 25393. OPEN 9.30 – 5.30 MON, 9 – 5.30
TUE – SAT, 11 – 4 SUN , 10 – 5 BANK HOLIDAYS
9-11 CHAPEL STREET, SOUTHPORT, MERSEYSIDE PR8 1AE
☎ (01704) 531583. OPEN 9 – 5.30 MON – SAT, 11 – 4
SUN, PHONE FOR BANK HOLIDAY OPENING TIMES.
Clarks International operate a chain of factory shops nationally which specialise in selling slight seconds and ends of lines from Clarks Shoes, K Shoes and other brands. These trade under the name of Crockers, K Factory shop or Clarks Factory Shop and while not all are physically attached to a shoe factory, these shops are treated as factory shops by the company. Customers can expect to find a wide choice of children's shoes for ages three upwards, from trainers, football boots and wellingtons to slippers and summer sandals. Brands stocked include Clarks,

K Shoes, Puma, Mercury, and Dr Martens although not all are sold in every outlet. Discounts are on average between 15%–35% off the normal high street price.

LAMBERT HOWARTH FOOTWEAR

GAGHILLS MILLS, BURNLEY ROAD EAST, WATERFOOT, ROSSENDALE, LANCASHIRE BB4 9AS
☎ (01706) 215417. OPEN 10 – 5 MON – FRI, 9.30 – 3.30 SAT, 10 – 5 BANK HOLIDAYS.
A real mixture of seconds from the factory and perfects from other sources. Seconds in footwear are from shoes made for BhS and C&A and all are at discounted prices. These include slippers, walking boots, flat shoes and sandals for children. There are also perfects in clothes from Italy, Spain and Portugal at two-thirds of the high street prices.

LAURA ASHLEY

HORNSEA FREEPORT SHOPPING VILLAGE, HORNSEA, YORKSHIRE HU18 1UT
☎ (01964) 536503. OPEN 10 – 5 MON – FRI, 10 – 6 SAT, SUN.
This factory shop is one of two dozen at the Hornsea Freeport Shopping Village. It sells children's clothes, mostly girls, from birth to nine years, all of which are Laura Ashley branded. There is also a home furnishings department which may stock children's curtain material and wallpaper. The shop looks just like an ordinary retail outlet. The shopping village has restaurants, play centres, a vintage car collection, water games, and plenty for the family to do.

Many art galleries and museums offer free workshops during the school holidays and at half term. They usually get booked up very early so make sure you find out about what your local venue is offering well in advance.

LAURA ASHLEY

BOUNDARY MILL, BURNLEY ROAD, COLNE, LANCASHIRE
☎ (01282) 860166. OPEN 10 – 6 MON – FRI, 10 – 5 SAT,
11 – 5 SUN.
This is basically a clearance outlet, selling women's and
children's clothes only (no home furnishings), mostly one or
two seasons old. Items are usually discounted by at least 40%.
There are no boys' clothes and only a limited selection for girls
including dresses, blouses, jumpers and trousers.

LIGHTWATER VALLEY FACTORY SHOPPING

NORTH STAINLEY, NEAR RIPON, YORKSHIRE HG4 3HT
☎ (01765) 635321. OPEN 10 – 6 SEVEN DAYS A WEEK.
Factory outlet complex set in the biggest leisure park in the north
of England with up to 50 companies selling discounted items. The
childrenswear range isn't large, but worth a trip for a day out
while visiting the trout pond, visitors' farm and coffee shop.

M C HITCHEN & SONS LTD

116 ST JAMES STREET, BURNLEY, LANCASHIRE BB11 1NL
☎ (01282) 425615. OPEN 9.30 – 5.30 MON – FRI, UNTIL
4.30 ON TUE, 9 – 5.30 SAT.
602-608 ATTERCLIFFE ROAD, SHEFFIELD,
SOUTH YORKSHIRE S9 3QS
☎ (0114) 2441611. OPEN 9.30 – 5.30 MON – SAT.
102 DEANSGATE, BOLTON, GREATER MANCHESTER
BL1 1BD
☎ (01204) 384969. OPEN 9.30 – 5.30 MON – WED,
9 – 5.30 THUR – SAT.
185 STAMFORD STREET, ASHTON UNDER LYME,
GREATER MANCHESTER OL6 7PY
☎ (0161) 339 0966. OPEN 9 – 5.30 MON – SAT, UNTIL
5.15 ON THUR.
160 MARINE ROAD, CENTRAL MORECAMBE,
LANCASHIRE LA4 4BU
☎ (01524) 412074. OPEN 9.30 – 5.30 MON, 9 – 5.30
TUE – SAT.

14-16 NORTH STREET, RUGBY, WARWICKSHIRE CV21 2AF
☎ (01788) 565116. OPEN 9.30 – 5.30 MON – WED,
9 – 5.30 THUR – SAT.
C/O LITTLEWOODS, SHOPPING CITY, RUNCORN, CHESHIRE
(01928) 717777. OPEN 9 – 5 MON – SAT.
69-74 LORD STREET, FLEETWOOD, LANCASHIRE FY7 6DS
☎ (01253) 773418. OPEN 9 – 5.30 MON – SAT

Littlewoods mail order catalogue sale shops, most of which are
in the north of England, offer up to 40% off the catalogue price
of clothing and between 50% and 60% off electrical goods.
They also run a mobile shop which operates in cities where they
don't have a sale shop. For details for future venues for the
mobile sales, which usually take place once a month, contact
Mrs Jean Banks, c/o Crosby DC, Kershaw Avenue, Endbutt
Lane, Crosby, Merseyside L70 1AH; (0151) 928 6611.

MADE TO LAST LTD

8 THE CRESCENT, HYDE PARK, LEEDS LS6 1BH
☎ (0113) 2304983. OPEN 10 – 6 TUE – SAT, CLOSED
MONS.

A workers co-operative making boots and shoes, they have
regular stock clearances during which shoes which have been
tried on by customers and don't look quite as new are reduced
in price by between one third and one half. Their children's
shoes took first prize in the 1993 Shoe and Sock Awards,
beating industry giants Start-Rite into second place. Their
children's boots normally cost £36.95, strap shoes, £42 and
classic men's lace-ups, £59. Send for catalogue. All their styles
are also available in a high quality vegetarian material. They
also offer a stretching service by post.

When knitting cardigans for a baby, make button-holes on both sides. After
the baby is born, you can simply stitch the buttons on the left or right, to
suit boy or girl.

MATALAN

HOLME ROAD, BAMBER BRIDGE, PRESTON,
LANCASHIRE PR5 6BP
☎ (01772) 627365. OPEN 10 – 8 MON – FRI, 9 – 6 SAT,
11 – 5 SUN.

UNIT 1, RED ROSE CENTRE, REGENT ROAD,
SALFORD M5 3GR
☎ (0161) 848 0792. OPEN 10 – 8 MON – FRI, 9 – 6 SAT,
11 – 5 SUN.

UNIT 29, GREYHOUND RETAIL PARK, SEALAND ROAD,
CHESTER CH1 1QG
☎ (01244) 380877. OPEN 10 – 8 MON – FRI, 9 – 6 SAT,
11 – 5 SUN.

UNIT 13, THE WHEATLEY CENTRE, WHEATLEY HALL ROAD,
DONCASTER DN2 4PE
☎ (01302) 760444. OPEN 10 – 8 MON – FRI, 9 – 6 SAT,
11 – 5 SUN.

UNIT 4B, STADIUM WAY RETAIL PARK, PARKGATE,
ROTHERHAM S60 1TG
☎ (01709) 780173. OPEN 10 – 8 MON – FRI, 9 – 6 SAT,
11 – 5 SUN.

UNITS 10 & 11, CLIFTON MOORE CENTRE, YORK YO3 4XZ
☎ (01904) 693080. OPEN 10 – 8 MON – FRI, 9 – 6 SAT,
11 – 5 SUN.

NEW CHESTER ROAD, BROMBOROUGH,
SOUTH WIRRAL L62 7EK
☎ (0151) 343 9494. OPEN 10   8 MON – FRI, 9 – 6 SAT,
11 – 5 SUN.

SEFTON RETAIL PARK, DUNNINGS BRIDGE ROAD, BOOTLE,
MERSEYSIDE L30 6UU
☎ (0151) 525 1190. OPEN 10 – 8 MON – FRI, 9 – 6 SAT,
11 – 5 SUN.

UNIT 3, ALEXANDRA CENTRE, OLDHAM,
LANCASHIRE OL4 1SG
☎ (0161) 620 6686. OPEN 10 – 8 MON – FRI, 9 – 6 SAT,
11 – 5 SUN.

UNIT 2, KINGSTONE RETAIL PARK, HULL HU2 2TX
☎ (01482) 586184. OPEN 10 – 8 MON – FRI, 9 – 6 SAT,
11 – 5 SUN.

WESTOVER STREET, OFF STATION ROAD, SWINTON,
LANCASHIRE M27 2AH
☎ (0161) 794 3441. OPEN 10 – 8 MON – FRI, 9 – 6 SAT,
11 – 5 SUN.

UNIT 1, GREENMOUNT RETAIL PARK, PELLON LANE,
HALIFAX HX1 5QN
☎ (01422) 383051. OPEN 10 – 8 MON – FRI, 9 – 6 SAT,
11 – 5 SUN.

UNIT 1, HEWITTS CIRCUS, CLEETHORPES,
SOUTH HUMBERSIDE DN35 9QH
☎ (01472) 200255. OPEN 10 – 8 MON – FRI, 9 – 6 SAT,
11 – 5 SUN.

DUDLEY ROAD, SCUNTHORPE DN16 1BA
☎ (01724) 270958. OPEN 10 – 8 MON – FRI, 9 – 6 SAT,
11 – 5 SUN.

UNIT 2, CLIFTON RETAIL PARK, CLIFTON ROAD,
BLACKPOOL FY4 4US
☎ (01253) 697850. OPEN 10 – 8 MON – FRI, 9 – 6 SAT,
11 – 5 SUN.

UNITS G & H, THE TRIUMPH CENTRE, HUNTS CROSS,
LIVERPOOL L24 9GB
☎ (0151) 486 0325. OPEN 10 – 8 MON – FRI, 9 – 6 SAT,
11 – 5 SUN.

A former cash and carry company, Matalan has now become a discount club operation which sells 90% clothing and 10% household items, toiletries and luggage at its 37 branches countrywide. Members are usually employees whose company is registered with Matalan, senior citizens with a pension through one of the listed companies, or anyone who is VAT-registered. But members of the public can gain access on a Thursday with a day pass. Merchandise is sold at between 20%–50% cheaper than high street prices. And unlike many discount club operations, you don't have to buy in bulk.

OPPORTUNITIES

13 Providence Street, Wakefield, West Yorkshire
WF1 3BG
☎ (01924) 290310 Open 10 – 5.30 Mon – Fri, 9 – 5.30
Sat, Until 7 Thur.
Two floors of nearly-new outfits, including a section of
babywear to clothes for children up to the age of twelve. Some
designer labels in the dresses, trousers, shoes and slippers. No
toys or baby equipment. Easy parking, easy sofas, and coffee
and tea served.

SCOOPS

Ingleby Road, Bradford Yorkshire BD99 2XE
☎ (01274) 521674. Open 10 – 5 Mon, 10 – 8 Tues – Sat.
Crown Point, Unit 9 Crown Point Retail Park,
Hunslett Road, Leeds
☎ (0113) 2341924. Open 10 – 5 Mon, 10 – 7 Tue – Fri,
9.30 – 6 Sat, 11 – 5 Sun.
Shirethorne Centre, 34-43 Prospect Street, Hull
HU2 8PX
☎ (01482) 224354. Open 9 – 5.30 Mon – Sat.
c/o Discount Giant, Brothers Street,
Blackburn BB2 4SY,
☎ (01254) 200449. Open 8.30 – 6 Mon – Wed,
8.30 – 8 Thur, Fri, 8.30 – 6 Sat, 10 – 4 Sun.
Sisson Street, Off Oldham Road, Failsworth M35 0EJ
☎ (0161) 6825684. Open 8.10 –8 Mon – Thurs,
8:30 – 9 Fri, 8.30 – 8 Sat, 10 – 4 Sun.
Grattan, the mail order company, use a chain of shops in the
North and Midlands to clear their overstocks. There is a
selection of items from those featured in the catalogue, which
can consist of anything from children's clothes and toys to
bedding, electrical equipment and nursery accessories. All
items are discounted by between 30% and 50%.

SOPHIE'S CHOICE

19B NORTH LANE, HEADINGLEY, LEEDS,
WEST YORKSHIRE 6LS6 3HW
☎ (0113) 2743913. OPEN 10 – 5 MON – SAT,
CLOSED WED.

Nearly-new children's and women's clothes including French and Italian makes from the ages of eighteen months to teenagers. Labels range from Marks & Spencer and Mothercare to Oilily and OshKosh.

THE ELITE DRESS AGENCY

35 KINGS STREET WEST, MANCHESTER M3 2PW
☎ (0161) 8323670. OPEN 9.30 – 5.30 MON – SAT.

Three floors of good quality nearly-new clothing, from babywear to adult sizes. There are also some ends of lines and bankrupt stock. Childrenswear tends to be the top end of the market with Baby Mini, Oilily, OshKosh and Nippers labels and ranges from dresses and shirts to coats and rainwear, but no footwear. There are also occasionally accessories such as cots, prams and pushchairs, depending on whether someone brings them in for sale.

THE FACTORY SHOP

THE AIRE VALLEY BUSINESS CENTRE, BEECH HOUSE,
LAWKHOLME LANE, KEIGHLEY, WEST YORKSHIRE BD21 3JQ
☎ (01535) 611703. OPEN 9.30 – 5 MON – SAT, 10 – 4
BANK HOLIDAYS.
THE FACTORY SHOP, LANCASTER LEISURE PARK,
WYRESDALE ROAD, LANCASTER, LANCASHIRE LA1 3LA
☎ (01524) 846079. OPEN 10 – 5 MON – SUN, 10 – 5 BANK
HOLIDAYS.
THE FACTORY SHOP, 5 NORTH STREET, RIPON,
NORTH YORKSHIRE HG4 1JY
☎ (01765) 601156. OPEN 9 – 5 MON – SAT, 11 – 4 BANK
HOLIDAYS.

THE FACTORY SHOP, HORNSEA FREEPORT SHOPPING
VILLAGE, HORNSEA, NORTH HUMBERSIDE HU18 2UD
☎ (01964) 534211. OPEN 10 – 5 SEVEN DAYS A WEEK
AND BANK HOLIDAYS.
LIGHTWATER VALLEY, NORTH STAINLEY, RIPON,
NORTH YORKSHIRE HG4 3HT
☎ (01765) 635438. OPEN 10 – 5 SEVEN DAYS A WEEK.
The Factory Shop carries a constantly changing variety of
infants' and children's clothing, footwear and accessories,
specialising in chainstore and branded ends of lines and slight
seconds. All the major store brands are carried from time to
time, with the age range covering birth to twelve years. New
deliveries are made weekly and in some cases daily, so it is
impossible to say what is in each store at any one time. All
merchandise is on sale at around one-third off the high street
prices, but customers have to be quick to get the best bargains.
Babywear is just one department – stores also stock Footwear,
Clothing, Household Goods, Toiletries and Bedding.

THE SHOE FACTORY SHOP

21 WELLOWGATE, GRIMSBY, SOUTH HUMBERSIDE
DN32 0RA
☎ (01472) 342415. OPEN 9 – 5 MON – SAT, 9 – 7 THUR.
Children's shoes from size 6 to adult size 5 from £10 upwards.
Slippers start at baby size 4 from £3.50–£6.50 to junior
size 2.

THE SHOE SHED

C/O CLOTHING WORLD, UNITS 10 AND 11,
WHEATLEY CENTRE, WHEATLEY HALL ROAD, DONCASTER,
YORKSHIRE DN2 4PE
Wide range of quality footwear at below retail prices. There are
no seconds – just perfects, as you would expect from a high
street store. They stock a variety of brand names such as Pebe
and Dunlop and for very young babies trying their first shoes,
Dandystepps. Sizes start from 2 and prices from £4.50. They
also stock their own quality shoes, The Jennings Collection –

prices start from £7.50 – and their Reflex range of sports shoes.
Staff are friendly and willing to help.

YOYO

61 EASTGATE, BEVERLEY, NORTH HUMBERSIDE HU17 0DR
☎ (01482) 861713. OPEN 9.30 – 3 MON – SAT.

Aimed at children, YoYo sell good quality, nearly-new
childrenswear from babies to twelve year olds at prices from
one quarter to one third of the original cost. The labels range
from Marks & Spencer, Debenhams and BhS to Oilily, Patrizia
Wigan, Tick Tock, Babi-Mini, Clayeaux and Absorba. There is
also a small selection of toys around Christmas, plus children's
bedding, and they operate a travel cot hire service.

MILUPA BABYFOOD

SCIENTIFIC DEPARTMENT, MILUPA HOUSE,
UXBRIDGE ROAD, HILLINGDON, MIDDLESEX UB10 0NE
☎ 0181-573 9966.

About to wean your baby? Test his or her taste buds without opening your
purse. Write to Milupa, who produce baby foods, with the date of birth of
your infant, and they will send you free samples at a time that is
appropriate to your baby's age.

NORTH AND SCOTLAND

BABYGRO LTD

HAYFIELD INDUSTRIAL ESTATE, KIRKCALDY, FIFE,
SCOTLAND KY2 5DN
☎ (01592) 261177. OPEN 10.30 – 4.30 MON, 9.30 – 4.30
TUE – SAT.
GATESIDE INDUSTRIAL ESTATE, OLD PERTH ROAD,
COWDEN BEATH
☎ (01383) 511105. OPEN 12 – 4.30 MON – WED,
9.30 – 4.30 THUR, 9.30 – 12.30 FRI.
Babywear for 0–5 year olds: all-in-ones, playsuits, shorts,
T-shirts, vests, shirts, pyjamas and rompers at factory shop
prices. Pyjamas for a 4-year-old cost £5.99 compared with
£12.99 for the same pair in a high street store. Factory sales take
place three times a year and are advertised locally. At time of
going to press, there were plans to expand the Kirkcaldy shop to
twice its size and include cot bedding as well as extending the
age range to seven years. Opening hours will probably also
expand so phone first.

BAIRDWEAR RACKE

9 – 13 NETHERDALE ROAD, NETHERTON INDUSTRIAL
ESTATE, NETHERTON, WISHAW, SCOTLAND
☎ (01698) 357231. OPEN 10 – 4 MON – THUR,
10 – 12 FRI.
6-8 COLVILLES PLACE, EAST KILBRIDE, GLASGOW,
SCOTLAND G75 0QS
☎ (01355) 236441. OPEN 10 – 4 MON – THUR,
10 – 12 FRI.
24 ROSYTH ROAD, POLMADIE, GLASGOW
☎ (0141) 429 6611. OPEN 11 – 4 MON – THUR,
9.30 – 12.30 FRI, CLOSED 2.30 – 3 DAILY.

INCHINNEN INDUSTRIAL ESTATE, ABBOTSBURN,
RENFREWSHIRE PA4 9RP
☎ (0141) 812 4085. OPEN 9.30 – 4.30 MON – WED,
9.30 – 2.15 THUR, 9.30 – 12.30 FRI.
The Wishaw outlet stocks mostly schoolwear – trousers, shorts,
pinafores, skirts – from the age of three upwards to size 34"
waist and 38" bust. Most items are about 40% less than normal
retail prices. The Glasgow outlet has a small selection of
Marks & Spencer seconds, mostly blouses, jackets and anoraks
for ages up to seven. The Polmadie outlet offers a complete
cross section of dresses, trousers, tracksuits, pyjamas but
no schoolwear. The Renfrewshire branch has a full range of
children's clothes: trousers, tracksuits, coats, pyjamas for ages
up to thirteen. Most have been made for well-known high street
department stores.

BARBOUR LTD

BEDE INDUSTRIAL ESTATE, SIMONSIDE, SOUTH SHIELDS,
TYNE & WEAR NE34 9PD
☎ (0191) 455 4444. OPEN 10 – 5 TUE – FRI, UNTIL 6 ON
THUR, 9 – 12 SAT.
The famous waterproof waxed jackets and outdoor wear, all of
which are seconds, at discounts of at least 15% from the factory
shop. Unfortunately, they don't carry a large stock of children's
sizes, but extra small 24" chest size jackets, large children's
waxed jackets in sage or navy and warm linings which can be
clipped onto the inside of jackets are usually available.

Buy new and secondhand books in good condition at sales held by
Amnesty International's British Section. Normally, a local Amnesty group
hires a hall and sets up stall with thousands of books on sale, many of
them publishers' review copies. Look up the telephone number of your local
Amnesty branch in the business telephone directory for your area and
check when the sale is on.

BURBERRY

KITTY BREWSTER INDUSTRIAL ESTATE, BLYTHE,
NORTHUMBERLAND
☎ (01670) 352524. OPEN 10 – 3.30 MON – THUR, 10 – 3
FRI, 9.30 – 12.30 SAT.

Most of the Burberry factory shops sell seconds and overmakes
of the famous name raincoats and duffle coats, as well as
accessories such as the distinctive umbrellas, scarves and
handbags, plus gift food items. All carry the Burberry label and
are about one third of the normal retail price. Childrenswear
tends to be thin on the ground, so phone before visiting.

CROCKERS

UNIT 26, THE FORGE SHOPPING CENTRE, PARKHEAD,
GLASGOW, SCOTLAND G31 4EB
☎ (0141) 556 5290. OPEN 9 – 5.30 MON – SAT, 12 – 5
SUN AND BANK HOLIDAYS.

Clarks International operate a chain of factory shops nationally
which specialise in selling slight seconds and ends of lines from
Clarks Shoes, K Shoes and other brands for children. These
trade under the name of Crockers, K Factory shop or Clarks
Factory Shop and while not all are physically attached to a shoe
factory, these shops are treated as factory shops by the
company. Customers can expect to find a wide choice of
children's shoes, from Clarks, K Shoes, Dr Martens and famous
name brands in trainers, although all are not sold in every
outlet. Discounts are on average around 30% off the normal
high street price for perfect stock.

Wear a perfume constantly while nursing the new baby in hospital and
continue to wear the same fragrance after you get home. Then when you
put the baby to bed, you can put a drop of that perfume on the sheet or
mattress (never put a pillow in a baby's cot) and the baby will associate
the smell with you, giving you an increased chance of an unbroken's
night's sleep.

FACTORY BEDDING AND FABRICS SHOP

ATLAS HOUSE, NELSON STREET, DENTON HOLME,
CARLISLE CA2 5NB
☎ (01228) 514703. OPEN 10 – 5.30 MON – FRI, 9 – 5 SAT,
PHONE FOR OPENING TIMES DURING BANK HOLIDAYS.
Bedding, cot quilts, cot blankets, cot sheets, curtains, duvets,
duvet covers, pillows, towels, cushions, baby wear and curtain
fabrics at factory shop prices. Towels have Disney designs from
the Lion King to Mickey Mouse, as well as the ubiquitous Mr
Blobby. Pillows from £1.99; handtowels, 75p; quilts from £5.99;
curtains from £10.99; fabrics from 75p a metre.

GARDINER OF SELKIRK

TWEED MILLS, SELKIRK, SCOTLAND TD7 5DZ
☎ (0750) 20283. OPEN 9 – 5 MON – SAT IN SUMMER,
10 – 4 IN WINTER.
Factory shop making textiles which also sells bought-in
products including jumpers from £10 for children aged up to
twelve.

I J DEWHIRST

MILL HILL, NORTH WEST INDUSTRIAL ESTATE, PETERLEE,
DURHAM SR8 1AT
☎ (0191) 586 4525. OPEN 9 – 7.30 MON – FRI, 9 – 5 SAT,
10 – 5 SUN.
PENNYWELL INDUSTRIAL ESTATE, PENNYWELL,
SUNDERLAND
☎ (0191) 534 7928. OPEN 9 – 5.30 MON – FRI, 9 – 5 SAT,
11 – 5 SUN, 9 – 5 BANK HOLIDAYS.
Manufactures clothing for various high street stores including
Marks & Spencer, although you won't find any M&S labels in
the outfits at their Peterlee and Pennywell factory shops as
anything that could identify them as such has to be cut out first.
There are lots of children's clothes, and some seconds in baby
and toddler wear. These include anoraks, schoolwear, girls'
dresses, boys' shirts, trousers, girls' nightwear, duffle coats and
girls' ski pants.

JACKSONS LANDING
THE HIGHLIGHT, HARTLEPOOL MARINA, HARTLEPOOL, DURHAM TS24 0XN
☎ (01429) 866989. OPEN 10 – 6 MON – SAT, 11 – 5 SUN AND BANK HOLIDAYS.

Factory shopping village which caters mostly for adults but does have some factory outlets selling merchandise for children at discounted prices including JoKids childrenswear and Toy World which sells Tomy, Fisher-Price and Lego. Some of the other shops such as Clinkards shoes do sell children's sizes, and Tog 24 has some small thermal wear and waterproofs. Children might also be tempted by the Sweet Temptations confectionary.

K SHOES
NETHERFIELD, KENDAL, CUMBRIA LA9 7BT
☎ (01539) 721892. OPEN 9.30 – 7 MON – FRI, 9 – 5 SAT, 11 – 5 SUN. 9.30 – 5 BANK HOLIDAYS.
MAIN STREET, SHAP, CUMBRIA CA10 3NL
☎ (01931) 716648. OPEN 9 – 5 MON – SAT, 10 – 5 BANK HOLIDAYS.

Clarks International operate a chain of factory shops nationally which specialise in selling slight seconds and ends of lines from Clarks Shoes, K Shoes and other brands for children. These trade under the name of Crockers, K Factory shop or Clarks Factory Shop and while not all are physically attached to a shoe factory, these shops are treated as factory shops by the company. Customers can expect to find a wide choice of children's shoes, from Clarks, K Shoes, Dr Martens and famous name brands in trainers, although all are not sold in every outlet. Discounts are on average around 30% off the normal high street price for perfect stock.

When washing a baby's or small child's hair, smear a little petroleum jelly above the eyebrows and this will stop water or suds running into the eyes as it should direct the suds to the side of the face.

KILNCRAIGS MILL

PATON & BADLWINS LTD, ALLOA, SCOTLAND FK10 1EG
☎ (01259) 723431. OPEN 10 – 4.30 MON – FRI, 10 – 4
SAT.

Sells a range of knitwear from babywear and pram covers to snowsuits, anoraks, pyjamas and cords, as well as Patons wool and discontinued yarns. Tapestries include Forever Friends and other nursery designs. Kilncraigs is a working mill with an on-site factory shop.

M C HITCHEN & SONS LTD

19 FAWCETT STREET, SUNDERLAND, TYNE & WEAR
SR1 1RH
☎ (0191) 564 0684. OPEN 8.45 – 5.30 MON – SAT.
RAWLINSON STREET, BARROW IN FURNESS, CUMBRIA
LA14 1BS
☎ (01229) 870668. OPEN 8.45 – 5.15 MON – SAT.

Littlewoods mail order catalogue sale shops, most of which are in the north of England, offer up to 40% off the catalogue price of clothing and between 50% and 60% off electrical goods. They also run a mobile shop which operates in cities where they don't have a sale shop. For details for future venues for the mobile sales, which usually take place once a month, contact Mrs Jean Banks, c/o Crosby DC, Kershaw Avenue, Endbutt Lane, Crosby, Merseyside L70 1AH; (0151) 928 6611.

MATALAN

16 GOODWOOD SQUARE, TEESIDE RETAIL PARK, THORNABY,
STOCKTON-ON-TEES TS17 7BW
☎ (01642) 633204. OPEN 10 – 8 MON – FRI, 9 – 6 SAT,
11 – 5 SUN.
SEAFIELD WAY, SEAFIELD ROAD, EDINBURGH EH15 1TB
☎ (0131) 657 5045. OPEN 10 – 8 MON – FRI, 9.30 – 5.30
SAT, 10 – 6 SUN.
WALNEY ROAD, BARROW LA14 5UN
☎ (01229) 430899. OPEN 10 – 8 MON – FRI, 9 – 6 SAT,
11 – 5 SUN.

UNIT 2B, METRO CENTRE RETAIL PARK, GATESHEAD, NEWCASTLE UPON TYNE NE11 4YD
☎ (0191) 460 0423. OPEN 10 – 8 MON – FRI, 9 – 6 SAT, 11 – 5 SUN.

UNIT 5, CALEDONIAN CENTRE, NEW ASHTREE STREET, WISHAW ML2 7UR
☎ (01698) 357075. OPEN 10 – 8 MON – FRI, 9.30 – 5.30 SAT, 10 – 6 SUN.

PLOT 12, DERWENT HOWE, SOLWAY ROAD, WORKINGTON, CUMBRIA CA14 3YA
☎ (01900) 870966. OPEN 10 – 8 MON – FRI, 9 – 6 SAT, 11 – 5 SUN.

UNIT 7, GLENCAIRN RETAIL PARK, KILMARNOCK, SCOTLAND KA1 4AY
☎ (01563) 73892. OPEN 10 – 8 MON – FRI, 9.30 – 5.30 SAT, 10 – 6 SUN.

A former cash and carry company, Matalan has now become a discount club operation which sells 90% clothing and 10% household items, toiletries and luggage at its 37 branches countrywide. Members are usually employees whose company is registered with Matalan, senior citizens with a pension through one of the listed companies, or anyone who is VAT-registered. But members of the public can gain access on a Thursday with a day pass. Merchandise is sold at between 20%–50% cheaper than high street prices. And unlike many discount club operations, you don't have to buy in bulk. There's a wide range of children's clothing, including jeans, denim jackets, coats, girls' dresses, jumpers and jogging suits, with more merchandise for babies and children under 9, although the age range does go up to about 12.

An American tip for clean sheets when trying to leave the nappy off your toddler overnight: make a sheet sandwich of a rubber sheet, a dry sheet, a rubber sheet, a dry sheet. When he or she wets the bed, just strip off the top set of wet sheet and rubber sheet, revealing the bottom dry set.

Q MARK
56 BELFORD ROAD, EDINBURGH, SCOTLAND EH4 3BR
☎ (0131) 225 6861. OPEN 9 – 5.30 MON – SAT, UNTIL 7 THUR.
BRAIDHOLM ROAD, GIFFNOCK, GLASGOW,
SCOTLAND G46 6EB
☎ (0141) 633 3636. OPEN 9 – 6 MON – SAT, UNTIL 8 ON THUR, 12 – 5 SUN.
Scotland's biggest discount clothing warehouse for children, women and men offers top quality fashions at up to 50% off normal high street prices. All garments are good quality seconds, overmakes or cancelled contracts but with their labels cut out. Regular stock deliveries ensure a constant selection of new styles – often recognised in famous chain stores, but always at ridiculously low prices. Q Mark operate a once-a-year membership fee of £5. All prices are subject to VAT which is charged at point of sale.

STATESIDE WHOLESALE CLUB
☎ (01670) 789110. MAIL ORDER THROUGH AN AGENT.
Contrary to what it might seem, this is not an American company. Based in Northumberland, it is a catalogue company with a trio of brochures featuring children's, men's and women's clothes which are left at your home. You can then order the various outfits through the agent who comes to collect the catalogue. The real bargains come if you are an agent, as you can then charge whatever price you like for the goods in the catalogue as long as you pay the company a fixed amount for each outfit. The catalogue states the normal retail price for each outfit, but the agent's price list states the amount the company wants from the agent for that item. This amount is often half the catalogue price. It suggests that you sell the outfit at its fixed price plus 20%. The company claims that all the merchandise is perfect, big brand names on sale currently in shops and other catalogues. You have to purchase something to get on the mailing list but once you start receiving catalogues, you can sell to friends or use it to buy clothes for yourself and your family at

low prices. The children's clothes are of the leggings and T-shirt variety.

THE FACTORY SHOP LTD
EMPIRE BUILDING, MAIN STREET, EGREMONT, CUMBRIA CA22 2BD
☎ (01946) 820434. OPEN 9 – 5 MON – SAT, 10 – 4 BANK HOLIDAYS.
The Factory Shop carries a constantly changing variety of infants' and children's clothing, footwear and accessories, specialising in chainstore and branded ends of lines and slight seconds. All the major store brands are carried from time to time, with the age range covering birth to 12 years. New deliveries are made weekly and in some cases daily, so it is impossible to say what is in each store at any one time. All merchandise is on sale at around one-third off the high street prices, but customers have to be quick to get the best bargains. Babywear is just one department – stores also stock Footwear, Clothing, Household Goods, Toiletries and Bedding.

TURNABOUT
32 PRIORY PLACE, CRAIGIE, PERTH, SCOTLAND
☎ (01738) 630916. OPEN 9.30 – 5 MON – FRI, 10 – 4 SAT.
Nearly-new children's clothes from birth to ten years, as well as equipment from high chairs, cots, prams and buggies to play pens and car seats. They also hire out baby equipment and at time of going to press were planning to sell new children's clothes made on the premises.

Planning a fund-raising event which will involve children? They love bouncy castles, but they're expensive to hire. Contact the country's leading building society, The Halifax, who will supply bouncy castles and the staff to man them for charitable events, as long as there are 1,000 people attending. Apply in writing to your local branch for details well in advance of the event as they tend to be very booked up.

NORTHERN IRELAND

DESMOND & SONS LTD
THE MAIN STREET, CLAUDY, LONDONDERRY BT47 3SD
☎ (01504) 338441. OPEN 9.39 – 5.30 MON – SAT.
Manufacturers for Marks & Spencer, the factory shop stocks a
wide range of childrenswear at discount prices from trousers,
dresses, coats, jeans, T-shirts and jackets to pyjamas and
tracksuits. There are no M&S socks or underwear, although
occasionally they also buy in stock from other factories which
may include the latter.

ELIZABETH ALEXANDRA
2 MOYBRICK ROAD, DROMARA, COUNTY DOWN BT25 2BT
☎ (01238) 532519. OPEN 8.15 – 5.15 MON – THUR,
8.15 – 1.15 FRI.
Seconds and ends of lines of mainly childrenswear at discounts
of between 25% and 50%. Jogging suits, sweatshirts, girls'
shorts, boys' trousers but no underwear. All are Elizabeth
Alexandra label clothes.

LEE APPAREL (UK) LTD
16 COMBER ROAD, NEWTOWNARDS,
COUNTY DOWN BT23 4HY
☎ (01247) 800200. OPEN 10 – 5.15 MON, TUE, WED, SAT,
10 – 8.15 THUR, FRI.
Children's Lee jeans, jackets, T-shirts, hats, and sweatshirts at
up to 50% savings for seconds and perfects.

OCTOPUS SPORTSWEAR MFG LTD
UNIT 1, DUBLIN ROAD INDUSTRIAL ESTATE,
STRABANE BT82 9EA
☎ (01504) 882320. OPEN 9 – 5 MON – FRI, 9 – 1 SAT.
Wide range of children's sportswear – but no babywear –
including tracksuits, football vests, boots and trainers at less
than the normal retail prices. Mostly for ages five to six.

REGATTA FASHIONS LTD

1 Ballycregagh Road, Cloughmills, Ballymena,
County Antrim BT44 9LD
☎ (012656) 38692. Open 10 – 4.30 Mon – Sat.
Children's fashions from trousers and shirts, plain jumpers and
anoraks to blouses and skirts, dresses and accessories at
discounts of between 15%–20%. Lots of babywear in stock.

RELIABLE HOSIERY

The Factory Shop, 41 High Bangor Road,
Donaghadee, County Down BT21 0PD
☎ (01247) 888842. Open 10 – 5 Mon – Sat.
Shaerf Drive, Saracen, Lurgan,
County Armagh BT66 8DE
☎ (01762) 329253. Open 10.30 – 4.30 Mon – Fri.
Full range of baby clothes, babygros, baby hats, nightwear, suits
and dresses. For children, there are shirts, dresses, trousers,
nightwear, and accessories as well as underwear. Most of the
stock was made for Marks & Spencer or Laura Ashley, but all
the labels are removed before being put on sale. Discounts are
up to 50%.

Most new mothers receive a Bounty Pack when they are in hospital after
giving birth. This contains samples and sometimes even full-size packs of a
wide range of products from baby lotion, wipes and shampoo to nappy
sacks, toothpaste, nappies and photographic discounts. It's useful for trying
out products before deciding whether they suit you and your baby. The new
mother pack also contains a Babycare book which has a claim card which
you can redeem at Boots the Chemist for a Baby Progress Pack when your
child is four months. This gives you products appropriate to your baby's
age such as baby food, drink, rusks, powdered meals, etc. The mothers of
more than 800,000 babies a year receive these packs.

DECORATING THE NURSERY

LONDON

ALEXANDER FURNISHINGS

51-61 WIGMORE STREET, LONDON W1H 9LF
☎ 0171-935 7806. OPEN 9 – 6 MON – SAT,
UNTIL 7 ON THUR.

The largest independent curtain retailer in the UK, Alexander Furnishings are famous for curtaining, and also sell upholstery fabric, wallpapers and carpets. There's usually a discount on all fabrics – which includes those with children's motifs. They also do nursery lampshades and cot accessories. If not in stock, items can be ordered from the catalogue.

ANTA

46 CRISPIN STREET, SPITALFIELDS, LONDON E1
☎ 071-247 1634. OPEN 11 – 3 MON – FRI.

Workshop which sells jazzy check woollen rugs, fabric and ceramics ends of lines at discounts of about 25%. 100% wool knee blankets are suitable for cots and the plaid rugs in pinks and blues would look lovely on nursery floors.

BY THE YARD

8-12 WINDMILL HILL, ENFIELD, MIDDLESEX EN2 6SA
☎ 0181-363 7768. OPEN 9 – 5.30 MON – SAT.

Soft furnishings and upholstery fabrics, which are imported, as well as wallpaper and blinds at discount. Holds two collections with cars and bunny rabbit designs as well as children's borders and wallpapers. Sanderson, Warner and Monkwell are just some of the other fabric names on offer. Some stock is carried, but usually you order after looking through the order books. Small purchases – say one metre of fabric – won't be heavily discounted as the cost of transporting the item from the manufacturer to the shop will wipe out most of the profit. So the larger your order, the bigger the discount, but it can be anything from 20%–40%.

CIDMAR

10 SPRINGBRIDGE ROAD, LONDON W5 2AA
☎ 0181-567 8188. OPEN 9 – 5 MON – SAT.
Cidmar holds large stocks of both plain and printed fabric, net curtain, curtain tracks, and poles – all at discounted prices. Most leading brand names are sold here and they offer a good range of children's fabrics and curtains featuring childish motifs. Ready to hang net curtains are marked down by 20%, glazed cotton at about half-price, and there is a standard 15% discount off curtain tracking.

CORCORAN & MAY

11 THE GREEN, HIGH STREET, LONDON W5 5DA
☎ 0181-567 4324. OPEN 10 – 5.30 MON – SAT.
157-161 LOWER RICHMOND ROAD, LONDON SW15 1HH
☎ 0181-788 9556. OPEN 10 – 5.30 MON – SAT.
Not a specialist children's furnishings shop, Corcoran & May sell seconds, overstocks and clearance from top designers including Monkwell, Colefax & Fowler and G P & J Baker. You will also find many of the best designs from some of the brightest newcomers. Their stock includes simple cream damask from Lancashire, checks and stripes from India, brightly coloured brocades from Italy, plus intricate floral prints in the great English tradition. I have used their star design fabric in my daughter's room – there is plenty of choice here, depending on your taste and how "childish" you want your children's rooms to be.

Many women's magazines now have pages of freebies. For example, one issue of *Practical Parenting* offered £4,000-worth of free gifts including 100 videos worth £9.99 each, and 50 bathtime kits worth £15 each. If you really don't want to spend any money, nip into your local largest newsagent where you won't be spotted noting down the details and then send in your name and address and hope you strike lucky. The winners are usually picked at random after a set closing date.

MAINLINE
UNITS 2 & 3, PASADENA CLOSE, PUMP LANE, HAYES,
MIDDLESEX UB3 3MQ
☎ FREEPHONE MAINLINE. OPEN 8.30 – 5.30 MON – FRI.
As exhibitions contractors, Mainline have excellent contacts
with carpet manufacturers from whom they buy huge quantities for their main business. Now, they are offering GDD
readers, both those in business and domestic users, the chance
to buy a wide range of brand new carpets from Berber to velvet
cords without the traditional markup of the wholesaler.
Mainline staff will visit your home, measure up, advise you on
the type of carpet you need and offer a fitting service. Because
they will fit at weekends or in the evenings, they're particularly
useful for people who run businesses and don't want work
disrupted during the day. They offer a countrywide service.
Phone the above number or call the operator and ask for
Freephone Mainline Exhibitions.

THE CURTAIN EXCHANGE
133 STEPHENDALE ROAD, LONDON SW6 2PG
☎ 0171-731 8316/7. OPEN 10 – 5 MON – SAT.
40 LEDBURY ROAD, LONDON W11 2AB
☎ 0171-229 4923. OPEN 10 – 5 MON – SAT.
The Curtain Exchange is a countrywide network of shops
selling top quality, nearly-new curtains, blinds, pelmets, etc at
between one-third and one half of the brand new price. While
they can't guarantee that they will stock nursery motif designs,
they usually have a good stock of brightly coloured and
patterned curtains and blinds. Their stock comes from a variety
of sources: people who are moving house and hate the drapes in
their new home; people who are moving house and want to sell
their old curtains to help with the bills; show houses, where the
builder wants to recoup some of his outgoings; interior
designers' mistakes. Designer names include Colefax & Fowler,
Designers Guild, Laura Ashley, Warner, Sanderson and
Osborne & Little.

THE CURTAIN MILL

46-52 FAIRFIELD ROAD, LONDON E3 2QB

☎ 0181-980 9000. OPEN 9 – 5.30 SEVEN DAYS A WEEK.

207-211 THE VALE, ACTON, LONDON W3 7QS

☎ 0181-743 2299. OPEN 9 – 5.30 SEVEN DAYS A WEEK.

Huge choice of top quality fabrics at really low prices – from 99p a metre and including excellent discounts on many designer labels. A large warehouse, it stocks quality fabrics in many designs, including nursery prints. There is a customer hotline on 0171-375 1000.

VICTOR OF ROMFORD

14 WESTERHAM ROAD, LEYTON LONDON E10 7AE

☎ 0181-532 8636. OPEN 10 – 6 MON – SAT, 10 – 3 SUN.

Sheeting, curtain fabrics, lining, wadding and patchwork at discount prices. Most of the sheeting and curtaining is clearance lines and seconds, although some stock is the result of buying in bulk and selling at very competitive prices. Brand names include Coloroll, Dorma and the occasional Designers Guild and there are designs suitable for children's rooms. They also operate a mail order service.

Some museums offer free entrance after a certain time of day, usually an hour or two before closing. The Imperial War Museum in Lambeth Road, London, for instance, is free after 4.30pm on weekdays and weekends, leaving you one and a half hours to enjoy the exhibitions. Check out your local museums.

SOUTH EAST

BOYNETT FABRICS CO LTD

2 Aston Road, Cambridge Road, Bedford,
Bedfordshire MK42 0JN
☎ (01234) 217788. Open 9.30 – 5 Mon – Fri.
Curtain fabrics manufactured by Boynett, who are wholesalers,
and sold in the factory shop at discount prices for seconds and
over-runs. Also a curtain-making service. There are savings of
50% on the children's and nursery ranges which are currently
being extended to include five new designs including a candy
stripe. Self-adhesive PVC, launched in 1995, will include
nursery designs and be ideal for use in children's rooms.

CORCORAN & MAY

1 St Botolph's Road, Sevenoaks, Kent TN13 3AJ
☎ (0732) 741851. Open 10 – 5.30 Mon – Sat.
Not a specialist children's furnishings shop, Corcoran & May sell
seconds, overstocks and clearance from top designers including
Monkwell, Colefax & Fowler and G P & J Baker. You will also find
many of the best designs from some of the brightest newcomers.
Their stock includes simple cream damask from Lancashire,
checks and stripes from India, brightly coloured brocades from
Italy, plus intricate floral prints in the great English tradition. I
have used their star design fabric in my daughter's room – there is
plenty of choice here, depending on your taste and how
"childish" you want your children's rooms to be.

CURTAIN UP

The Annexe, Fifehead Manor Hotel, Middle Wallop,
Hampshire SO20 8EG
☎ (01264) 781244. Open 2 – 5 Mon, Wed, Thur,
10 – 1 Sat, And By Appointment.
Out of town small but packed shop selling top quality and
designer secondhand curtains and accessories at a fraction of

their original cost. There are no children's curtains as such with childish motifs, but many customers buy primary coloured curtains for their children's rooms. Stock changes constantly and there are always more than 75 sets of curtains in fabric names such as Colefax & Fowler, Osborne & Little, Designers Guild, Bakers, Warners, Laura Ashley and Crowsons. Many curtains are new and range from a small pair for £20 to large grand ones for £400. The setting is delightful in a building adjacent to a lovely hotel which can offer tea, coffee, lunch, etc, for those making a longer journey.

FABRIC WORLD

287-289 HIGH STREET, SUTTON, SURREY SM1 1LL
☎ 0181-643 5127. OPEN 9 – 5.30 MON – SAT.
6-10 BRIGHTON ROAD, SOUTH CROYDON,
SURREY CR2 6AA
☎ 0181-688 6282. OPEN 9 – 5.30 MON – SAT.
A family business which specialises in buying job lots and "parcels" from designer houses such as Designers Guild and Osborne & Little, as well as an enormous amount of French and Italian fabrics. These are all perfect goods and sell from between £6 and £13 per metre. There are always around 6,000 rolls in stock at any one time, and they offer a comprehensive making up service. They do stock specific motifs for children from time to time, but it is not a major part of their business.

G P & J BAKER AND PARKERTEX

PO BOX 30, WEST END ROAD, OFF DESBOROUGH ROAD,
HIGH WYCOMBE, BUCKINGHAMSHIRE HP11 2QD
☎ (01494) 467400. OPEN 9 – 1 SAT.
Mainly discontinued lines, but also some seconds, of these famous-name furnishing fabrics and curtaining. Prices range from £3.95 to £16.95, with the normal retail price marked on a board nearby so you can see what you're saving.

GOLDPINE OF SUSSEX LIMITED

HACKHURST LANE, LOWER DICKER,
EAST SUSSEX BN27 4BW
☎ (01323) 845353. OPEN 10 – 4 SEVEN DAYS A WEEK.
13 FRYER ARCADE, WINCHESTER ROAD, CHANDLERS FORD,
HAMPSHIRE
☎ (01703) 262929. OPEN 10 – 6 MON – SAT. PHONE
FIRST.

A family firm who for three generations have been making solid pine (including bases of drawers and backs of cabinets) furniture, Goldpine now has four factory shops (see under South East and North West) where you can order Goldpine furniture directly, saving 30% on retail prices. Their wide range includes a small bed which can be painted or carved and a small wardrobe with two drawers which is very popular for children. There is a massive range to choose from and you can feel at home with your choice for 21 days before deciding to keep it. All furniture is fully guaranteed. Send for the free mail order brochure. Free nationwide mainline delivery.

GRANDFORD CARPET MILLS

UNIT 11, BRIDGE INDUSTRIES, BROAD CUT, FAREHAM,
HAMPSHIRE
☎ (01329) 289612. OPEN 9 – 5 MON – FRI, 10 – 4 SAT.
Good quality carpets at half the price you would pay in high street shops.

KNICKERBEAN

11 HOLYWELL HILL, ST ALBANS, HERTFORDSHIRE AL1 1EZ
☎ (01727) 866662. OPEN 9 – 5.30 MON – SAT.
87 HIGH STREET, TUNBRIDGE WELLS, KENT TN1 1XZ
☎ (01892) 520883. OPEN 9 – 5.30 MON – SAT.
8 BARTHOLOMEW STREET, NEWBURY, BERKSHIRE RG14 5LL
☎ (01635) 529016. OPEN 9 – 5.30 MON – SAT.

This is the fabric company that concentrates on finding ends of lines, manufacturers' overstocks and slight seconds, which are sold at around half the original recommended retail price, sometimes even less. Thousands of metres are in stock, priced between £5.95 and £15.95 a metre, including a selection of fabrics suitable for children's playrooms and bedrooms. But these fabrics move so fast that the trick is when you see something you like, not to deliberate too long, as they are often not repeatable. If sewing or creative homemaking is not your forte, Knickerbean's portfolio of excellent design ideas and first-class making up service could ensure your new nursery is completed within three to four weeks.

SUE FOSTER FABRICS

57 HIGH STREET, EMSWORTH, HAMPSHIRE PO10 7YA
☎ (01243) 378831. OPEN 9.30 – 5 MON – FRI,
9.30 – 1 WED, SAT.
Supplies top name furnishing fabrics at discounts. She does hold books of children's fabrics and wallpapers with animal motifs and coloured patterns. Her showroom has one of the widest range of pattern books outside London, where customers can choose perfect fabrics and wallpapers, usually 15–20% below retail price. Also takes orders and sends out samples and undertakes sample searches – send for the questionnaire. The discount depends on the quantity bought.

THE CURTAIN CONNECTION

108A LONDON ROAD, ST ALBANS, HERTFORDSHIRE
☎ (01727) 868368. OPEN 10 – 2.30 TUE – FRI, 9.30 – 5 SAT.
Secondhand curtains and soft furnishings with lots of designer remnants from labels such as Designers Guild, Warners, Sanderson and Laura Ashley. Usually one-third of the original price, The Curtain Connection is affiliated to The Curtain Group, a series of independently owned and operated businesses which work together for publicity and which will contact each other with a customer's requests if they do not have your specific requirements in stock.

THE CURTAIN EXCHANGE

SHOP 3, 194 MAXWELL ROAD, BEACONSFIELD,
BUCKINGHAMSHIRE HP9 1QX
☎ (01494) 680662. OPEN 9.30 – 4.30 TUE – SAT.
NAGS CORNER (A134), WISTON ROAD, NAYLAND,
NR COLCHESTER, ESSEX CO6 4LT
☎ (01206) 263660. OPEN 10 – 4 MON – SAT.
45 HIGH STREET, CUCKFIELD, WEST SUSSEX RH17 5JU
(01444) 417000. OPEN 10 – 4 TUE – SAT.

The Curtain Exchange is a countrywide network of shops selling top quality, nearly-new curtains, blinds, pelmets, etc at between one-third and one half of the brand new price. While they can't guarantee that they will stock nursery motif designs, they usually have a good stock of brightly coloured and patterned curtains and blinds. Their stock comes from a variety of sources: people who are moving house and hate the drapes in their new home; people who are moving house and want to sell their old curtains to help with the bills; show houses, where the builder wants to recoup some of his outgoings; interior designers' mistakes. Designer names include Colefax & Fowler, Designers Guild, Laura Ashley, Warner, Sanderson and Osborne & Little.

THE CURTAIN MILL

21 GREYCAINE ROAD, WATFORD,
HERTFORDSHIRE WD3 4DS
☎ (01923) 220339. OPEN 9 – 5.30 SEVEN DAYS A WEEK.

Huge choice of top quality fabrics at really low prices – from 99p a metre and including excellent discounts on many designer labels. A large warehouse, it stocks Wilson Wilcox, Maria Collins, and discontinued lines of Blendworth, among other leading names at discount prices. It does stock some material which is suitable for nurseries and children's rooms. There is a customer hotline on 0171-375 1000.

SOUTH WEST

CAVE INTERIORS
MOUSEPLATT, SIDBURY, SIDMOUTH, DEVON EX10 0QE
☎ (01395) 597384. OPEN BY APPOINTMENT ONLY.
Specialists in discontinued and seconds designer fabrics, Cave Interiors sells everything from florals to stripes and checks, chintzes, printed cottons and kilims so there should be plenty of choice for children's rooms. Ramm Son & Crocker, Monkwell, and Bundles Designs are among the well known designers regularly stocked. The majority of fabric, which normally sells for in excess of £15 a metre, will cost from £8–£10 a metre.

JUST FABRICS
THE BRIDEWELL, DOCKACRE ROAD, LAUNCESTON,
CORNWALL PL15 7YZ
☎ (01566) 776279. OPEN 9 – 5.30 MON – SAT. AND MAIL ORDER.
Based in a large showroom in a former warehouse approached through an open courtyard, Just Fabrics hold the largest sample library in the country for all types of furnishing fabrics and wallpapers, which includes several ranges of specific children's fabrics and wallpapers, as well as quilts made to order. All the top brand names are represented and there is a discount of between 20%–25% off the recommended retail prices of most items. The company undertakes to despatch the goods to customers on receipt of the order, and says that distance is no object. They also have a mail order catalogue of their bedlinen and patchwork quilts.

Never use bottles that originally contained soft drinks to store anything else. Small children may identify the bottles as harmless and help themselves to a drink.

KNICKERBEAN

5 WALCOT STREET, BATH, AVON BA1 5BN
☎ (01225) 445741. OPEN 9 – 5.30 MON – SAT.

This is the fabric company that concentrates on finding ends of lines, manufacturers' overstocks and slight seconds, which are sold at around half the original recommended retail price, sometimes even less. Thousands of metres are in stock, priced between £5.95 and £15.95 a metre, including a selection of fabrics suitable for children's playrooms and bedrooms. But these fabrics move so fast that the trick is when you see something you like, not to deliberate too long, as they are often not repeatable. If sewing or creative homemaking is not your forte, Knickerbean's portfolio of excellent design ideas and first-class making up service could ensure your new nursery is completed within three to four weeks.

LOOSE ENDS

GILES GREEN, BRINKWORTH, CHIPPENHAM,
WILTSHIRE SN15 5DQ
☎ (01666) 510815. OPEN 9 – 1 MON – FRI OR BY APPOINTMENT.

Operating from two large converted barns in the grounds of the proprietor's house, Loose Ends offers top quality discontinued lines of fabric and textured and plain upholstery fabrics which they obtain from the best houses in London and New York and sell at about one third of the normal price. They hold very large stocks of all types of furnishing fabrics including lining, interlining and wallpapers which you can buy on the spot.

The Donkey Sanctuary near Sidmouth, Devon, is home to more than 400 retired or ill-treated donkeys. Many are former beach donkeys, others are victims of cruelty. There are guided tours of the donkey sanctuary with case histories of some of the incumbents, and visitors are free to roam at will and stroke the donkeys. There is no entrance charge. The Sanctuary is located on the A3052 Exeter to Lyme Regis road, near Sitford. Phone 01395 516391.

THE CURTAIN EXCHANGE

1ST FLOOR, 123 HIGH STREET, MARLBOROUGH,
WILTSHIRE SN8 1LZ
☎ (01672) 516994, OPEN 10 – 4 TUE – SAT.
LONGALLER MILL, BISHOP'S HULL, TAUNTON,
SOMERSET TA4 1AD
☎ (01823) 326071. OPEN 10 – 4 WED – SAT OR BY
APPOINTMENT.

The Curtain Exchange is a countrywide network of shops
selling top quality, nearly-new curtains, blinds, pelmets, etc at
between one-third and one half of the brand new price. The
Marlborough branch does get nursery curtains fairly frequently,
but turnover is fast. But while they can't guarantee that they will
stock nursery motif designs, they usually have a good stock of
brightly coloured and patterned curtains and blinds. Their stock
comes from a variety of sources: people who are moving house
and hate the drapes in their new home; people who are moving
house and want to sell their old curtains to help with the bills;
show houses, where the builder wants to recoup some of his
outgoings; interior designers' mistakes. Designer names include
Colefax & Fowler, Designers Guild, Laura Ashley, Warner,
Sanderson and Osborne & Little.

THE CURTAIN TRADING COMPANY,

ROUNDWAY FARM, DEVIZES, WILTSHIRE SN10 2HU
☎ (01380) 723113. OPEN 9.30 – 2.30 TUE, THUR,
9.30 – 1 SAT, AND BY APPOINTMENT.

Top quality and designer secondhand curtains and blinds,
some of which are brand new samples or designer mistakes.
Occasionally, they have specific nursery patterns, but a
good selection of their stock is suitable for children's
rooms.

If your baby suffers from nappy rash, apply a coating of egg white – it is
soothing as well as healing.

THE MAGNIFICENT MATERIAL COMPANY

188 Tytherington, Nr Warminster,
Wiltshire BA12 7AD
☎ (01985) 840870. (01985) 850501. Open 9.30 – 12.30
Mon And Thur And By Appointment.

Sells fabric seconds, discontinued and ends of lines, as well as a few firsts from a converted barn in Wiltshire. Designer labels include Fischbacher, Colefax & Fowler, Jane Churchill, Monkwell and GP & J Baker and there is usually a reasonable selection of children's fabrics.

THE WILTON ROYAL WEAVERS SHOP

The Wilton Royal Carpet Factory, King Street (A36),
Wilton, Nr Salisbury, Wiltshire
☎ (01722) 742733. Open 9 – 5 Mon – Sat,
11 – 5 Sunday.

Slightly flawed, end of roll and remnants of Royal Wilton carpets at about 40% off. Bigger reductions for smaller pieces. Special offers at certain times. Can supply cheap and cheerful carpets for playrooms – ring to enquire.

Buy a child's car seat from Kwik Fit and if returned in good condition, your money will be refunded. This is particularly useful for parents who opt for a car seat which only lasts until their baby is about nine months old, rather than a seat which can be used until the age of four or five, by which time it will almost certainly be too grubby to exchange. Check Yellow Pages for your local supplier.

WALES AND WEST MIDLANDS

ABAKHAN FABRICS

COAST ROAD, MOSTYN, CLWYD CH8 9DX
☎ (01745) 560312. OPEN 9 – 5 SEVEN DAYS A WEEK,
UNTIL 8 ON THUR.

Abakhan is able to offer bargains on a vast range of curtain fabric, sheeting and novelty prints through bulk buying, or selling clearance lines, job lots and seconds. They usually stock fabric with designs featuring nursery rhyme characters, animals, Beatrix Potter or whatever the current trend is. They also stock fabric for bridesmaids' dresses. There is a gift shop selling reasonably priced John Adams toys, games, and soft toys, as well as a coffee shop and free parking at the Clwyd outlet. The Manchester and Liverpool outlets do not have free parking facilities.

CARPETS OF WORTH LTD

SEVERN VALLEY MILLS, SEVERN ROAD, STOURPORT-ON-SEVERN, WORCERSTERSHIRE DH13 9HA
☎ (01299) 827222. OPEN 9 – 5 MON – FRI, 8 – 12 SAT.

Sells Axminster carpets and rugs, both patterned or plain. These are usually seconds or overmakes, discontinued lines or end of contract rolls. Stock Stainmaster and Scotchgard protected carpets which would be particularly suitable for children's rooms.

Museum of Science and Industry in Birmingham is on three levels with an aircraft section featuring a Spitfire and a Hurricane; a fire arms section with guns on display, as well as locomotives and trams; and a large engineering hall with a science section with computers and toys. There are lots of hands-on activities and entrance is free. The Museum is at Newhall Street, Birmingham. Phone (0121) 235 1661.

EARLY'S OF WITNEY

MILL STREET, WITNEY, OXFORDSHIRE OX8 5EB
☎ (01993) 703131. OPEN 10 – 4 MON – FRI, 9 – 2 SAT.
Cot and pram blankets, in acrylic or pure new Merino wool,
some of which are satin bound, single duvets but no duvet
covers or bedlinen specifically for children. However, there
were plenty of single sheets and bedspreads when we visited,
with about 40% off the patchwork quilted bedspreads and 60%
off slightly marked seconds. Mainly own brand and Witney
Point seconds at factory prices.

GAYLINE LTD

LLWYNYPIA ROAD, TONYPANDY, MID GLAMORGAN,
WALES CF40 2ET
☎ (01443) 433454. OPEN 9 – 5 MON – SAT,
9.30 – 12.30 SAT, CLOSED 1 – 1.30 DAILY.
Specialise in blinds of all types which they sell by mail order.
Made to measure vertical blinds are available at 50% less than
normal retail prices, as are Venetian blinds. Other styles cost
20% less than normal retail prices. Children's designs are not in
the catalogue, but samples will be posted to you on request.
There is no charge for the catalogue.

JUST FABRICS

BURFORD ANTIQUES CENTRE, CHELTENHAM ROAD,
BURFORD, OXFORDSHIRE OX8 4JA
☎ (01993) 823391. OPEN 9.30 – 5.30 MON – SAT,
2 – 5 SUN. MAIL ORDER.
No relation to the company of the same name in Cornwall, Just
Fabrics has a clearance outlet selling some current lines, but
mostly last season's stock at correspondingly low prices. It also
has a mail order arm called Plain Fabrics by Post on (0993)
823690 so you can see samples. Children's motif fabrics, which
do not constitute the majority of the stock, are usually priced
between £4.95 and £8.95 a metre.

STEWART SECONDS

12 PIER STREET, ABERYSTWYTH, DYFED, WALES
☎ (01970) 611437. OPEN 9 – 5.30 MON – SAT,
11 – 5 SUN IN SUMMER.
14 NOTT SQUARE, CARMARTHEN, DYFED, WALES
☎ (01297) 222294. OPEN 9 – 5.30 MON – SAT.
HARFORD SQUARE, LAMPETER, DYFED, WALES
☎ (01570) 422205. OPEN 9.30 – 5.30 MON – SAT.
Y MAES, PWLLHELI, GWYNEDD, NORTH WALES
☎ (01758) 701130. OPEN 9 – 5.30 MON – SAT.

Branded merchandise from most of the major UK chain stores, all well-known high street department store names at half the retail store price. Clothes range from babywear to young teenage outfits, and there is also bedding for babies and for older children, towels and some soft toys. The Gwynedd branch does not stock a lot of bedding for children.

TARLETON MILLS FACTORY SHOP

C/O KWIKSAVE SHOPPING MALL, NANTHALL ROAD,
PRESTATYN, CLWYD, WALES LL19 9LR
NO PHONE. OPEN 8.30 – 5.30 MON, TUE, SAT,
8.30 – 8 WED, THUR, FRI, 10 – 4 SUN.

Owned by the Tarleton Mill Factory, there are three factory shops (see Wales and East Anglia) which only sell merchandise which is manufactured by Tarleton. They operate as completely separate concessions within Kwik Save stores in order to keep costs and therefore prices down. Tarleton Mill make household textiles for major high street stores and use only top quality fabrics. The shops sell children's duvet sets with circus and farmyard designs, bean bags, floor cushions and occasionally shaped animal cushions. All stock is either quality seconds or discontinued lines, for example cotton curtains from £6 to £50; piped cushion cover, £2.

Never leave plastic bags lying around where children can reach them.

THE ABBEY WOOLLEN MILL

MARITIME AND INDUSTRIAL MUSEUM, MARITIME QUARTER,
SWANSEA, WALES SA1 1SN
☎ (0792) 650351. OPEN 10.30 – 5.10 TUE – SUN.
Sells pure wool cot blankets in rose, pale blue and lilac, which
are satin bound, as well as knitting wool packs, Arran jumper
patterns and wool packs for size 22" upwards, all at between
30% and 50% cheaper than the same items in the high street.

THE CURTAIN AGENCY

GLOESTONE COURT HOTEL, GLOWSTONE, ROSS-ON-WYE,
HEREFORDSHIRE HR9 6AW
☎ (01989) 770367. OPEN 10 – 3 WED – SAT.
The Curtain Agency is affiliated to The Curtain Group, a series
of independently-owned and operated businesses which work
together for publicity and which will contact each other with
customers' requests if they do not have your specific require-
ment in stock. All the shops sell top quality and designer
secondhand curtains and blinds, but some of them also sell
gifts, children's clothes and fabric. This outlet does stock
children's fabrics, curtains and blinds, together with at least 75
pairs of curtains in fabrics such as Osborne & Little, Hill &
Knowles, Parkertex and Laura Ashley. Some of the curtains are
brand new samples or designer mistakes. The Curtain Agency
also sells fabrics, remnants, blinds and cushions. As we were
going to press, the Agency was about to re-locate, so do ring
before visiting to find out their new address.

THE CURTAIN BROKERS

THE GREY HOUSE, BURFORD ROAD, FILKINS,
NEAR LECHLADE, GLOUCESTERSHIRE GL7 3JW
☎ (01367) 860362. BY APPOINTMENT ONLY, VERY
FLEXIBLE.
The Curtain Brokers is an independently-owned and operated
business which sells top quality and designer secondhand
curtains and blinds, some of which are suitable for nurseries
and children's rooms. There are usually at least 75 pairs of

curtains in stock in fabrics such as Osborne & Little, Hill & Knowles, Parkertex and Laura Ashley. Some of the curtains are brand new samples or designer mistakes.

THE CURTAIN EXCHANGE

SHIPTON SOLLARS MANOR, SHIPTON SOLLARS,
NR. CHELTENHAM, GLOUCESTERSHIRE GL54 4HU
☎ (01242) 820100. OPEN 10 – 3 WED – SAT OR BY
APPOINTMENT.

The Curtain Exchange is a countrywide network of shops selling top quality, nearly-new curtains, blinds, pelmets, etc at between one-third and one half of the brand new price. They do stock curtains and blinds for children's nurseries and bedrooms fairly frequently but these sell very quickly indeed. But while they can't guarantee that they will stock nursery motif designs, they usually have a good stock of brightly coloured and patterned curtains and blinds. Their stock comes from a variety of sources: people who are moving house and hate the drapes in their new home; people who are moving house and want to sell their old curtains to help with the bills; show houses, where the builder wants to recoup some of his outgoings; interior designers' mistakes. Designer names include Colefax & Fowler, Designers Guild, Laura Ashley, Warner, Sanderson and Osborne & Little.

THE CURTAIN RACK

25 HIGH STREET, PERSHORE, WORCESTERSHIRE WR10 1AA
☎ (01386) 556105. OPEN 10 – 4.30 MON – FRI,
9.30 – 5.30 SAT.

Three showrooms with secondhand designer curtains at about one third of the price as new and ranging from £4 to £1,200 a pair. While they seldom stock nursery designs, there are often brightly coloured curtains which would be suitable for children's rooms.

TOP SERVICE

CHURCH END HOUSE, WHICHFORD, SHIPSTON ON STOUR, WARWICKSHIRE CV36 5PG

☎ (01608) 684829. OPEN BY APPOINTMENT ONLY. MAIL ORDER.

Mail order discount fabric, curtain trimmings, furnishing material and wallpaper service, all perfects. There is no catalogue; you choose your nursery fabrics from an ordinary high street outlet, noting designer name and design title, and ring Top Service to order at reduced prices.

TRADING UP

THE BRICKYARD, PRESTON-ON-STOUR, STRATFORD-UPON-AVON, WARWICKSHIRE CV37 8BN

☎ (01789) 450988. OPEN 10 – 4 WED – SAT.

In the attic of a barn, Trading Up is lined with fabrics like a bedouin tent. Ranging from as-new designer rejects to the softly-faded elegance of old linens and brocades, the stock of secondhand curtains is always changing, offering discerning customers the opportunity to obtain high quality soft furnishings at approximately one third of new prices. While nursery designs are not always in stock, there is plenty of choice from brightly coloured and patterned curtains for children's rooms. Curtain poles, blinds and accessories are also available. Run by an interior designer, advice comes free.

VOGUE CARPETS

11 BRUNSWICK STREET, NEWCASTLE UNDER LYME, STAFFORDSHIRE ST5 1HF

☎ (01782) 630569. OPEN 9 – 5.30 MON – SAT, CLOSED 12 ON THUR.

All types and styles of carpets at trade prices including stripes or coloured dot patterns for children's rooms at less than normal retail prices. Nationwide delivery £15.

EAST ANGLIA AND
EAST MIDLANDS

CLOTH MARKET
STAMFORD WALK, ST MARY'S STREET, STAMFORD,
LINCOLNSHIRE
☎ (01780) 64715. OPEN 9.30 – 5 MON – SAT,
CLOSED THUR.
Well-loved little shop selling upholstery and furnishing fabric
by Liberty, Sanderson, G P & J Baker, Monkwell and other good
quality makes.

COURTAULDS MERIDIAN
HAYDON ROAD, NOTTINGHAM, NOTTINGHAMSHIRE
☎ (0115) 9246100. OPEN 9 – 5 MON – FRI,
9 – 5.30 SAT.
Zorbit baby range for the nursery: cot quilts, pram quilts,
duvets, curtains and lamp shades. Also some children's
bedding with Peter Pan and Mr Blobby designs. Large range of
children's clothes from 12 months to about seven or eight years.
Plus there is a coffee shop on site and a car park.

CREATIVE CARPETS LTD
UNIT 8, MILL HILL INDUSTRIAL ESTATE, QUARRY LANE,
ENDERBY, LEICESTERSHIRE LE9 5AU
☎ (0116) 2841455. OPEN 9 – 3 SAT ONLY, WEEKDAYS BY
APPOINTMENT ONLY. CLOSED FIRST TWO WEEKS JULY AND
CHRISTMAS.
Genuine factory shop where all the goods are made on the
premises and sold in a corner of the 1,200 sq ft factory. All
carpets are heavy domestic 80/20 wool nylon, hessian backed
and velvet pile. There are many colours as well as plains,
Berbers and tweeds. Savings of 50% can be made by buying
direct from the factory.

FABRIC DESIGN

10-12 NORTH PARADE, MATLOCK BATH,
DERBYSHIRE DE4 3NS
☎ (01629) 584747. OPEN 1 – 5 MON, THUR, SUN,
10 – 5 TUE, WED, FRI, SAT.
Discount fabric shop which, while not catering specifically
for children, has plenty of striped fabric, colourful floral
designs and checks which would be suitable for children's
rooms. Buy in two metre lengths and the price is only £3.75
a metre.

KNICKERBEAN

66 OUT NORTHGATE STREET, BURY ST EDMUNDS,
SUFFOLK IP33 1JQ
☎ (01284) 704055. OPEN 9 – 5.30 MON – SAT.
This is the fabric company that concentrates on finding ends of
lines, manufacturers' overstocks and slight seconds, which are
sold at around half the original recommended retail price,
sometimes even less. Thousands of metres are in stock, priced
between £5.95 and £15.95 a metre, including a selection of
fabrics suitable for children's playrooms and bedrooms. But
these fabrics move so fast that the trick is when you see
something you like, not to deliberate too long, as they are often
not repeatable. If sewing or creative homemaking is not your
forte, Knickerbean's portfolio of excellent design ideas and first-
class making up service could ensure your new nursery is
completed within three to four weeks.

LINCOLN CLOTH MARKET

83 BAILGATE, LINCOLN, LINCOLNSHIRE LN1 3AR
☎ (01522) 529872. OPEN 9.30 – 5.30 MON – SAT,
11 – 4 BANK HOLIDAYS.
Stocking Jane Churchill, Ramm Son & Crocker, Christian
Fischbacher, Mulberry, Harlequin, curtains, border wallpaper
and dress fabrics and cottons, they usually have clearance and
discontinued lines at advantageous prices. While not stocking
anything specifically for children's rooms, many customers find

fabrics here which they use for curtains and upholstery in their nurseries.

PARTRIDGE & PEAR TREE

6 PARK LANE, NEWMARKET, SUFFOLK CB8 8AX
☎ (01638) 560438. OPEN 9.30 – 5.30 MON – SAT,
CLOSED THUR.

Two storey shop full to the brim with designer and furnishing fabrics and trimmings at up to one fifth of their normal retail prices. There are four or five ranges of children's fabrics including Monkwell from £6.95 a metre. Stock – which mostly consists of bankrupt merchandise, seconds, ends of lines and clearance – is constantly changing. Fabrics usually include chintz, damasks, linen unions, weaves and silks by top designer names. Will also do designs on headboards and pelmets for children's rooms.

TARLETON MILLS FACTORY SHOP

C/O KWIKSAVE, 540-570 SHEFFIELD ROAD, WHITTINGTON
MOOR, CHESTERFIELD, DERBYSHIRE S41 8LX
☎ (10246) 456726. OPEN 8.30 – 5.30 MON, TUE, SAT,
8.30 – 8 WED, THUR, FRI, 10 – 4 SUN.

Owned by the Tarleton Mill Factory, there are three factory shops (see Wales and East Anglia) which only sell merchandise which is manufactured by Tarleton. They operate as completely separate concessions within Kwik Save stores in order to keep costs and therefore prices down. Tarleton Mill make household textiles for major high street stores and use only top quality fabrics. The shops sell children's duvet sets with circus and farmyard designs, bean bags, floor cushions and occasionally shaped animal cushions. All stock is either quality seconds or discontinued lines.

Before removing a child's plaster, rub it with cotton wool dipped in baby oil – it won't hurt them so much.

THE CURTAIN MILL

ST GEORGE'S MILLS, HUMBERSTONE ROAD, LEICESTER,
LEICESTERSHIRE LE1 1SN
☎ (0116) 2620264. OPEN 9 – 5.30 MON – SAT,
9 – 5.30 SUN.

Huge choice of top quality fabrics at really low prices – from 99p
a metre and including excellent discounts on many designer
labels. A large warehouse, it stocks Wilson Wilcox, Maria
Collins, and discontinued lines of Blendworth, among other
leading names at discount prices. It does stock some material
which is suitable for nurseries and children's rooms. There is a
customer hotline on 0171-375 1000.

WATERSIDE MILL SHOP

359 SHEFFIELD ROAD, WHITTINGTON MOOR,
CHESTERFIELD, DERBYSHIRE S41 8LQ
☎ (01246) 456886. 0246 456752 FAX.
OPEN 9.30 – 5 MON – SAT, 10 – 4 SUN.

Very large outlet selling soft furnishing fabrics – some on
complete rolls, others as remnants – and also bedding fabrics
from names such as Dorma and Rose and Hubble. Thousands of
metres of top quality designs and chainstore seconds, all at
unbeatable prices. Stocks cot quilt panels and wadding to make
up and usually has a selection of children's fabrics and bedding.
Parking is easy.

Fenland Aviation Museum features engines, uniforms, aeroplanes such as
the Vampire T11 Jet Trainer, and Lightning Aircraft, parachutes and Thirties
and Forties memorabilia. Entrance is only 50p for adults and 25p for
children. It is situated in Bambers Garden Centre, where there is an aquatic
centre and tea room and is open weekends and bank holidays only.
Bambers Garden Centre is on Old Lynn Road, West Walton, Wisbech,
Cambridgeshire. Phone 01945 585808.

NORTH WEST, YORKSHIRE AND HUMBERSIDE

ABAKHAN FABRICS
111-115 OLDHAM STREET, MANCHESTER
☎ (0161) 839 3229. OPEN 9.30 – 5 MON – SAT, UNTIL
7.30 ON THUR, 11 – 4 SUN.
34-44 STAFFORD STREET, LIVERPOOL
☎ (0151) 207 4029. OPEN 9.30 – 5 MON – SAT.
8-12 GREENWAY ROAD, BIRKENHEAD, LANCASHIRE
☎ (0151) 652 5195. OPEN 9 – 5 MON – SAT, UNTIL 8 ON
THUR AND FRI, 11 – 4 SUN.
65-67 CHURCH ROAD, BIRKENHEAD, LANCASHIRE
☎ (0151) 652 6983. OPEN 9 – 5 MON – SAT.
Abakhan is able to offer bargains on a vast range of curtain
fabric, sheeting and novelty prints through bulk buying, or
selling clearance lines, job lots and seconds. They usually stock
fabric with designs featuring nursery rhyme characters, animals, Beatrix Potter or whatever the current trend is. They also
stock fabric for bridesmaids' dresses. There is a gift shop selling
reasonably priced John Adams toys, games, and soft toys, as
well as a coffee shop and free parking at the Clwyd outlet. The
Manchester and Liverpool outlets do not have free parking
facilities.

ASHTONS
NEWTON STREET, HYDE
☎ (0161) 368 1961. 9.30 – 1 FIRST SATURDAY OF EVERY
MONTH.
Baby's bedding, towelling nappies, towels, cot quilts, sheets,
robes, pram quilts, nursery curtains and matching duvets,
pillows, sheets, all at competitive prices.

ASTBURY LIGHTING LTD
FOUNDRY BANK, CONGLETON, CHESHIRE
☎ (01260) 278114. OPEN 10 – 5 MON – SAT AND BANK
HOLIDAYS.
Factory shop situated in an old mill selling lamp shades –
patterned and plain bases and shades and wall lighting from
£10–£100. Most of the stock is seconds and is reduced by about
one-third. In another part of the building, bedding, curtains and
clothes are sold.

BABYWORLD
HALLAM MILL, HALLAM STREET, HEAVILEY, STOCKPORT
☎ (0161) 4779999. OPEN 9.30 – 5 MON – SAT.
WARWICK MILL, OLDHAM ROAD, MIDDLETON
☎ (0161) 6537117. OPEN 9 – 5 MON – SAT.
Babyworld has two branches, both of which sell nursery
equipment and decorative and soft furnishing accessories.
The latter are made by the factory at the Middleton site and
are therefore sold in the shops at rock-bottom prices. These
include cot quilts and sheets, pram sheets, bumper sets,
changing bags, foot muffs, curtains, lamp shades, nappy
stackers and cot tidies. The company is also main agents for
Mamas & Papas, Cosatto, Maclaren, Chicco, Bebe Confort,
Cumfifolda and many more leading names and sells their
prams, pushchairs, cots, travel cots and car seats at very
competitive prices.

BROOKS MILL
SOUTH LANE, ELLAND, NR HALIFAX, YORKSHIRE
☎ (01422) 377337. OPEN 9.30 – 5.30 SEVEN DAYS A
WEEK.
Clearance outlet for Ponden Mills merchandise including
cot quilts, single bed sheets, duvets and bedding, with
various designs such as Thomas the Tank Engine and the Lion
King.

COURTAULDS TEXTILES

TRENCHERFIELD MILL, THE PIER, WIGAN, LANCASHIRE
☎ (01942) 39531. OPEN 9.15 – 4.30 MON – FRI,
10 – 3.30 SAT.

Part of the Pier complex, this factory outlet stocks only bedding and textiles. It carries the Zorbit baby range: cot and pram quilts, sheets and blankets, curtains, lampshades. Also children's bedding, manufactured for Marks & Spencer, including single bed sets with Mickey Mouse, Lion King, Sonic the Hedgehog and Dinosaur designs.

E G INTERIOR FABRICS

226 HARROGATE ROAD, CHAPEL ALLERTON,
LEEDS LS7 4QD
☎ (0113) 2370447. OPEN 9.30 – 5 MON – SAT,
CLOSED WED.
89 BRADFORD ROAD, EAST ARDSLEY, WAKEFIELD WF3 JQD
☎ (01924) 820593. OPEN OPEN 9.30 – 5 MON – SAT,
CLOSED TUE.

Sell curtaining, sheeting fabrics and curtain linings, specialising in wider widths, most of which are ends of lines, seconds and overprints of well-known chain store designs at savings of up to 50%. Sometimes have novelty prints such as nursery rhymes, but there are plenty of candy stripes, jazzy designs and navy, green and red patterns for children's rooms. Both shops offer a making up service.

FACTORY FABRICS FROM THE MILL SHOP

102 PIONEER HOUSE, NORTHGATE, DEWSBURY,
WEST YORKSHIRE WF15
☎ (01924) 459740. OPEN 9 – 5 MON – FRI,
9 – 4 SAT.

High street outlet measuring 800 sq ft selling curtain and upholstery fabrics from many well-known high street brands. Most goods are first quality. The majority of goods are priced in the range of £3.99 to £5.00 a metre. At time of going to press, they had puppet and harlequin design ranges for children, but with more than 12,000 metres to choose from, there must be something suitable here!

GOLDPINE OF SUSSEX LIMITED

6 EARL STREET, MOORFOOT, SHEFFIELD
☎ (0114) 2769229. OPEN 9.30 – 6 MON – SAT,
11 – 4 SUN.

A family firm who for three generations have been making solid pine (including bases of drawers and backs of cabinets) furniture, Goldpine now has four factory shops (see under South East and North West) where you can order Goldpine furniture directly, saving 30% on retail prices. Their wide range includes a small bed which can be painted or carved and a small wardrobe with two drawers which is very popular for children. There is a massive range to choose from and you can feel at home with your choice for 21 days before deciding to keep it. All furniture is fully guaranteed. Send for the free mail order brochure. Free nationwide mainline delivery.

MATERIAL THINGS

38 CHARLOTTE STREET, CHESHIRE,
MACCLESFIELD SK11 6JB
☎ (01625) 428923. OPEN 9.30 – 5 MON, TUE,
10 – 5 WED, 9.30 – 5.30 THURS, FRI, SAT.

Sells seconds, fents (small sections of 2 metres in length) and perfect ends of lines of furnishing and upholstery fabrics from designers such as Warners, Colefax & Fowler and Jane Churchill, among other top fabric designer names at very cheap prices. The material from which the fents come would normally cost about £15–£25 a metre; here, fents are sold at £7.50 each. Upholstery fabric costs £10 a metre, about one third of the normal price. Lots of bright, colourful fabrics but only a small selection of specific nursery prints.

SEYMOUR'S WAREHOUSE
1 EAST ROW, DARLINGTON DL1 5PZ
☎ (01325) 355272. OPEN 9 – 5 MON – SAT.
Trading in Darlington for more than 30 years, this warehouse
sells the best makes of household linens, including Dorma, at
discounted prices, as well as clearance lines in towels and
pillows. They usually have a good selection of children's
bedding including Peter Pan and Forever Friends design duvets.

SKOPOS MILL SHOP
COLBECK HOUSE, BRADFORD ROAD, BATLEY,
YORKSHIRE WF17 6LZ
☎ (01924) 475756. OPEN 9.30 – 5.30 MON – FRI,
9 – 5.30 SAT, 10 – 4.30 SUN.
SALTS MILL, VICTORIA ROAD, SALTAIRE,
SHIPLEY BD18 3LB
☎ (01274) 581121. OPEN 10 – 6 SEVEN DAYS A WEEK.
DAISY MILL, STOCKPORT ROAD, LONG SIGHT,
MANCHESTER M13 0LF
☎ (0161) 273 7120. OPEN 9.30 – 5 MON – FRI,
9.30 – 6 SAT, 10 – 4 SUN.
One of the world's leading designers and manufacturers of
furnishing fabrics, you can now buy many of these superb
ranges at substantial savings. There are fabrics with children's
designs in a range of five colourings, beans bags and floor
cushions. At their Yorkshire mill, they design and manufacture
flame retardant fabrics for leading international hotel groups
and interior designers. They now offer end of contract runs,
specials and quality seconds direct to the public. Ends of rolls
are half price, plus there are 100% cotton furnishing fabrics,
sheers, voiles and linings, ex-contract and ex-display curtains,
quilted bedspreads, quilted pieces, polycotton duvets and
sheets, cushions, haberdashery and remnants. The furniture
showroom on the ground floor of the Batley outlet, as well as
offering a wide range of sofas and chairs, also sells ex-display
and prototype models at greatly reduced prices. All three
branches offer the same bargains.

TARLETON MILLS FACTORY SHOP

C/O KWIKSAVE, 177 TOWNGATE, LEYLAND, NEAR PRESTON,
LANCASHIRE PR5 1TE
☎ (01772) 457696. OPEN 8.30 – 6 MON, TUE, SAT,
8.30 – 8 WED, THUR, FRI.
Owned by the Tarleton Mill Factory, there are three factory
shops (see Wales and East Anglia) which only sell merchandise
which is manufactured by Tarleton. They operate as completely
separate concessions within Kwik Save stores in order to keep
costs and therefore prices down. Tarleton Mill make household
textiles for major high street stores and uses only top quality
fabrics. The shops sell children's duvet sets with circus and
farmyard designs, bean bags, floor cushions and occasionally
shaped animal cushions. All stock is either quality seconds or
discontinued lines.

THE CURTAIN EXCHANGE

3 HAWTHORN LANE, WILMSLOW, CHESHIRE SK9 1AQ
☎ (01625) 536060 OPEN 10 – 5 MON – SAT.
The Curtain Exchange is a countrywide network of shops
selling top quality, nearly-new curtains, blinds, pelmets, etc at
between one-third and one half of the brand new price. They do
stock curtains and blinds for children's nurseries and bedrooms
fairly frequently but these sell very quickly indeed. But while
they can't guarantee that they will stock nursery motif designs,
they usually have a good stock of brightly coloured and
patterned curtains and blinds. Their stock comes from a variety
of sources: people who are moving house and hate the drapes in
their new home; people who are moving house and want to sell
their old curtains to help with the bills; show houses, where the
builder wants to recoup some of his outgoings; interior
designers' mistakes. Designer names include Colefax & Fowler,
Designers Guild, Laura Ashley, Warner, Sanderson and
Osborne & Little.

THE CURTAIN TRANSFER LTD

TEWIT WELL ROAD, OFF SOUTH DRIVE, HARROGATE,
NORTH YORKSHIRE HG2 8JF
☎ (01423) 505520. OPEN 10 – 4.30 TUE – SAT

Curtain Transfer has been trading in Harrogate for more than two years. There is always a good selection of long curtains, many of which are interlined, and a computerised stock list, updated daily, can be mailed out on request. They sell a lot of curtains for children's rooms, though not necessarily with nursery designs. Easy parking, plus there are plans to have spacehoppers and hop scotch and other traditional games to keep children occupied while parents browse at their leisure.

THE FABRIC SHOP

82 MAIN STREET, ADDINGHAM, NEAR ILKLEY,
YORKSHIRE LS29 0PL
☎ (01943) 830982. OPEN 10 – 6 MON, 9 – 1 TUE, WED,
FRI, 12 – 4 THUR AND SAT.

Great fabric bargains in this rabbit warren of interconnecting rooms, stacked high to the ceiling with bolts of perfects and seconds of furnishing fabrics. There are a few specific children's designs, and no fabric costs more than £10 a metre.

WATERSIDE MILL SHOP

CLARENCE MILL, CANAL SIDE, CLARENCE ROAD,
BOLLINGTON, CHESHIRE SK10 5JZ
☎ (01625) 576443. OPEN 9.30 – 5 MON – SAT,
10 – 4 SUN AND BANK HOLIDAYS.

Very large outlet selling soft furnishing fabrics – some on complete rolls, others as remnants – and also bedding fabrics from names such as Dorma and Rose and Hubble. Thousands of metres of top quality designs and chainstore seconds, all at unbeatable prices. Full making up service on the premises. Also available: various dress fabrics, towelling, leatherette, PVC, damask, corduroy, fleece, muslin, waddings, woollens, blanketing and haberdashery. Parking is easy.

NORTH AND SCOTLAND

J & W CARPETS
3 RUTHERGLEN ROAD, RUTHERGLEN, GLASGOW, SCOTLAND
☎ (0141) 647 9442. OPEN 9 – 8 MON – FRI, 9 – 5.30 SAT,
12 – 5 SUN.
UNIT 1, FORGE STREET UNITS, (OFF BONNYTON ROAD),
KILMARNOCK, SCOTLAND
☎ (01563) 35397. OPEN 9 – 8 MON – FRI, 9 – 5.30 SAT,
12 – 5 SUN.
24 BACK MAIN STREET, AYR, SCOTLAND
☎ (01292) 265539. OPEN 9 – 8 MON – FRI, 9 – 5.30 SAT,
12 – 5 SUN AND BANK HOLIDAYS.
Sells clearance lines and ends of rolls from £1 per sq metre, and
Axminster patterns for £2–£2.50 per sq metre, some suitable for
nurseries and playrooms. Stocks thousands of roll ends to fit
rooms of all sizes as well as 3,000 rolls of carpet in a variety of
sizes, colours and quality.

JENNY CLARKE FABRICS
CHURCH STREET, WINDERMERE, CUMBRIA LA23 1AQ
☎ (015394) 44686. OPEN 9 – 5 MON – FRI.
Mail order fabric discounters, curtaining and upholstery only,
including specific children's designs as well as other patterns
that are suitable for children's rooms. Usually about 25%
discount.

LONHRO TEXTILES
NELSON WAY, NELSON INDUSTIRAL ESTATE,
CRAMLINGTON, NORTHUMBERLAND NE23 9JT
☎ (01670) 713434. OPEN 9 – 5 MON – FRI, 9.30 – 4 SAT.
Perfect seconds and reject bedlinen, some with children's
designs such as clowns and kaleidoscope, as well as curtains.
Quilt cover sets are about £15.99 and there are often special
offers.

McALPIN & CO LTD

CUMMERSDALE PRINT WORKS, CARLISLE,
CUMBRIA CA2 6BT
☎ (01228) 25224. OPEN 9 – 4.30 MON – FRI, 10 – 4 SAT.
Factory shop selling seconds in linen, cotton, satin and
upholstery fabric as well as cushions. Some of the fabric is
slightly faulty. Children's motifs and brightly coloured stripes
are available at certain times. Everything is about half the
normal retail price. Free car parking.

SEKERS FABRICS

HENSINGHAM, WHITEHAVEN, CUMBRIA CA28 8TR
☎ (01946) 692691. PHONE FOR SALE TIMES.
Discontinued curtain and upholstery fabrics sold off at monthly
sales. Only open to the public during the sales – phone for
dates.

THE BED FACTORY

LEYDEN GARDENS, MERRYHILL, GLASGOW G20 9TP
☎ (0141) 945 0178. OPEN 8.30 – 4.30 MON – FRI,
9 – 4 SAT, 11 – 4 SUN.
Manufactures on the premises and so can sell at below retail
price. It stocks all sizes, shapes and styles of bed and can also
make to order, including bunk beds. Delivery service is
available over the whole of Scotland.

THE COTTON PRINT FACTORY SHOP

58 ADMIRAL STREET, GLASGOW G41 1HU
☎ (0141) 420 1855. OPEN 9.30 – 4.30 MON – SAT.
Large outlet selling cotton fabric, curtains, heading tapes, tie-
backs, curtain pulls, track fabrics at anything from 95p to £5.95
a metre. Lots of nursery designs and patterns for children
available.

THE CURTAIN EXCHANGE

30 JAMAICA STREET, GLASGOW G1 4QD
☎ (0141) 221 1070. OPEN 10 – 5 TUE – SAT.

The Curtain Exchange is a countrywide network of shops selling top quality, nearly-new curtains, blinds, pelmets, etc at between one-third and one half of the brand new price. While they can't guarantee that they will stock nursery motif designs, they usually have a good stock of brightly coloured and patterned curtains and blinds. Their stock comes from a variety of sources: people who are moving house and hate the drapes in their new home; people who are moving house and want to sell their old curtains to help with the bills; show houses, where the builder wants to recoup some of his outgoings; interior designers' mistakes. Designer names include Colefax & Fowler, Designers Guild, Laura Ashley, Warner, Sanderson and Osborne & Little.

NORTHERN IRELAND

CV HOME FURNISHINGS
OLD BLEACH WORKS, 36 MAGHERALANE ROAD,
RANDALSTOWN, ANTRIM BT41 2NT
☎ (018494) 72213. OPEN 10 – 5 MON – THUR, 10 – 1 FRI,
5.30 – 8 FIRST THUR OF EACH MONTH.
Factory shop selling home furnishings, including quilt covers
and pillow case sets with designs from Disney, Power Rangers,
Mickey and Minnie Mouse and other famous nursery characters. Most of the stock are grade 2s with a small number of
perfects.

School project material can be found free if you know where to look. If your
child is studying tea producing areas or nutrition you can get free leaflets
from the Tea Council and many of the supermarkets and manufacturers.
Contact the Tea Council for colourful posters telling where tea comes from
and how it is harvested on 0171-248 1024. Sainsbury's supermarket has a
freephone student line on 0800 387504. Tesco runs a Careline on 0800
505555. John West Foods Ltd sends out information packs – write to the
Marketing Department at West House, Bixteth Street, Liverpool L3 9SR or
phone (0151) 236 8771.

EQUIPMENT, SPORT AND LEISURE

LONDON

BABYCARE LTD

74 HIGH STREET, ACTON, LONDON W3 6LE
☎ 0181-993 8542. OPEN 10.15 – 5.30 MON – SAT.
Toys, baby feeding equipment, premature baby clothes,
nursery equipment including prams, cots and pushchairs from
Mamas & Papas and Silver Cross at prices which are lower than
those in department stores. Babycare advertise the fact that they
will beat anybody else's price. There is also a repair workshop
for the manufacturers they stock: Maclaren, Britax and Bebe
Confort.

BIBLIOPHILE BOOKS

21 JACOB STREET, LONDON SE1 2BG
☎ 0171-232 1927. MAIL ORDER.
Mail order books for children, as well as for adults, at half price
or less. Stock is brand new, remaindered. You can visit the
premises and purchase books.

CHILDREN'S PARTY HIRE

☎ 0181-952 8130. PHONE FIRST.
Everything you need for a successful celebration – except for the
entertainer. Based in the Stanmore, Middlesex, area, a small
charge is made for delivery. Examples of prices include three
tables and 14 chairs, £6; six tables and 26 chairs, £10.

FIRST SPORT BLACKS

456-458 THE STRAND, LONDON WC2R 0RG
☎ 0171-839 5161. OPEN 9.30 – 6 MON – WED, SAT,
9.30 – 7 THUR, FRI.
They are so certain that their prices for top brand-name sports
shoes are the lowest you will find that they guarantee that if you
buy from them and then see the same shoes cheaper elsewhere,
they will refund the difference. Brand names on sale at

discounts of up to 50% include Nike, Reebok, Puma and Adidas. The shop also sells children's ski all-in-ones and sticks, but no boots, brand name trainers or football strips.

LETTERBOX LIBRARY

2ND FLOOR, LEROY HOUSE, 436 ESSEX ROAD,
LONDON N1 3QP
☎ 0171-226 1633. MAIL ORDER.
Run by a women's co-operative, Letterbox offers non-sexist, non racist, multi-cultural books, as well as those about the environment and disabilty, for children up to the age of 14. Books are sold at discounts of between 10%–25%. Life membership is £5 and there are four or five members' sale days a year at the London headquarters.

RAINBOW

249 & 253 ARCHWAY ROAD, LONDON N6
☎ 0181-340 8003. OPEN 10.30 – 5 MON,
10.30 – 5.30 TUE – SAT.
Number 249 sells secondhand items, while 253 is new merchandise. Nearly-new consists of a wide range of well-known baby and children's clothes – from OshKosh and Oilily to Baby Gap and Marks & Spencer – as well as good condition baby equipment from cots and high chairs to car seats and playpens. They also sell secondhand toys (Galt and Fisher-Price), including a lot of traditional wooden toys such as Brio wooden trains, and books. The new shop sells a wide range of children's clothes, mainly in natural fabrics, and the imported items are discounted by about 12.5%. There are twice-yearly sales in January and July when prices are discounted further.

SWALLOWS & AMAZONS

91 NIGHTINGALE LANE, LONDON SW12 8NX
☎ 0181-673 0275. OPEN 10 – 5 MON – SAT.
Swallows & Amazons, now more than a decade old, now stock new travel cots, playpens and umbrella buggies at very competitive prices, as well as selling secondhand toys, books

and baby equipment in the basement. The ground floor is full of quality clothes for 0–12 year olds including Jacardi, Oilily, Jean le Bourget, OshKosh and Gap.

THE BABY'S ROOM
173 ST JOHN'S HILL, WANDSWORTH, LONDON SW11
☎ 0171-924 4711. OPEN 10 – 6 MON – SAT, 11 – 3 SUN.
Specialising in infants and tiny tots up to the age of three, it sells mostly secondhand nursery equipment, curtains, linen and toys with a small selection of clothing of labels such as Marks & Spencer, Next, Gap and Jonelle. Prices are usually at least half the normal retail price, depending on the condition of the item. They also hire out cots and prams.

TUTTI FRUTTI DISCOUNT STORE
156-158 RYE LANE, PECKHAM, LONDON SE15 4NB
☎ 0171-732 9933. OPEN 9 – 6 MON – SAT.
Nursery equipment shop which offers bigger discounts the more you buy and particularly if you pay cash. There are often special offers – buggies from £20, cots for £100. They stock all leading makes, as well as babywear, shoes, baby accessories, bedding, bath sets, textiles, feeding equipment, and have a repair service and a mail order facility. There are baby changing facilities in the shop and toys to play with.

WINKIE JANE
184 MUNSTER ROAD, FULHAM, LONDON SW6 6AU
☎ 071-384 1762. OPEN 9 – 5.30 MON – FRI, 10 – 5 SAT.
Good quality nearly-new car seats, buggies, prams, wooden toy boxes, Designers Guild quilts, baby Dior samples and unwanted gifts, as new. There is also children's clothing in this child-friendly shop with its big double doors for easy access with buggies and a toy box for children to play with while parents browse. There is on-street parking right outside and the clothes are well presented and uncluttered. Age range covered is 0–10.

SOUTH EAST

BABYCARE LTD
2 NEWMARKET SQUARE, TOWN CENTRE, BASINGSTOKE, HAMPSHIRE
☎ (0256) 330728. OPEN 9.30 – 5.15 MON – SAT.
Toys, baby feeding equipment, premature baby clothes, nursery equipment including prams, cots and pushchairs from Mamas & Papas and Silver Cross at prices which are lower than those in department stores. Babycare advertise the fact that they will beat anybody else's price. There is also a repair workshop for the manufacturers they stock: Maclaren, Britax and Bebe Confort.

BAGGINS BOOK BAZAAR
19 HIGH STREET, ROCHESTER, KENT ME1 1QB
☎ (01634) 811651. OPEN 10 – 6 SEVEN DAYS A WEEK.
Large selection of children's books, secondhand and review copies, for all ages, including some famous classic and collectors' items such as Rupert Bear annuals.

BARNADO'S
94 HIGH STREET, ROCHESTER, KENT ME1 1JT
☎ (01634) 831843. OPEN 9 – 5 MON – SAT.
Everything secondhand from clothes from birth to 14 years, to toys. There is a toy fair every year – ring for details.

CARGO CLUB
8 HESTERMAN WAY, VALLEY PARK, OFF PURLEY WAY, CROYDON, SURREY CR0 4YA
☎ 0181-686 9944. OPEN 10 – 8 MON – WED, 10 – 9 THUR, FRI, 10 – 7 SAT, 10 – 6 SUN.
A family means bigger food bills and anything that can help defray the costs is welcome. Cargo Club is a British-owned warehouse club which is open to members only, but membership is not very restrictive. You have to be either VAT registered

or a member of a certain profession – ring your local outlet for membership details. There is an enormous range of goods from brand name foods – Heinz baked beans, Coca Cola, butter, cheese, toilet paper, breakfast cereals – plus fresh meat, clothes, games, books, computers, camcorders, bedroom furniture, high chairs, playpens, toddler's beds and mattresses. All are very competitively priced indeed, although you may have to buy packs of four or more of food items.

COSTCO

WEST THURROCK WAY, WEST THURROCK,
ESSEX RM16 1WY
☎ (01708) 860557. OPEN 10 – 8.30 MON – FRI,
9 – 6.30 SAT, 11 – 5 SUN.
HARTSPRING LANE, BUSHEY, WATFORD,
HERTFORDSHIRE WD2 8JS
☎ (01923) 225449. OPEN AS ABOVE.
A members-only discount warehouse, specialising in food but also selling everything from computers and TVs, washing machines and cameras to books and clothes. There is plenty here for hard-pressed parents. Apart from the savings on tins of baked beans and fish fingers, there are children's clothes and discounted books, plus computer games and other electronic equipment for older offspring. You have to be VAT-registered or a member of a certain profession to join, although this is not a cash & carry and is open to individual members of the public. Phone head office on (01923) 213113 for membership details.

GOOSEBERRY BUSH

2 BARNHAM ROAD, BARNHAM, NR BOGNOR REGIS,
WEST SUSSEX PO22 0ES
☎ (01243) 554552 OPEN 10 – 4 MON – SAT
Stock ranges from a secondhand children's cots, toys, bedding and high chairs to a good selection of nearly-new maternity wear, children's wellingtons, slippers and tracksuits. New items can be found for very reasonable prices. Caters for children 0–10 years. Friendly atmosphere.

NIPPERS

Mansers, Nizels Lane, Hildenborough,
Kent TN11 8NX
☎ (01732) 838333/832243. Opening Hours Vary So
Phone First.
Chalkpit Farm, School Lane, Bekesbourne,
Canterbury, Kent CT4 5EU
☎ (01227) 832006. (01227) 831496 Fax.
Coddimoor Farm, Whaddon, Milton Keynes,
Buckinghamshire MK17 0IR
☎ (01908) 504506. (0908) 505636 Fax.
Whites Farm Bures Road, White Colne, Colchester,
Essex CO6 2QF
☎ (01787) 228000. (07187) 228560 Fax.

Nippers, the nursery equipment and toy specialists, started with a very clever and simple idea and have now built it up to create an award-winning chain of franchises. The company operates from converted barns on farms around the country, offering easy parking, no queues, and personal service. This is on top of competitive prices on prams, cots, pushchairs, car seats, outdoor play equipment and toys. Prices are low partly because they operate from farms, with none of the overheads of traditional retail outlets, and party because the successful growth of a number of branches means it can now buy in bulk and negotiate good deals. Customers can try out the merchandise and the children can see the animals, mostly sheep and pigs. Familiar brand names are on sale at all the branches, including Britax and Bebe Confort, Fisher-Price and Little Tikes. You can try out the car seats in your car and there is usually a pram/pushchair repair service on site.

If you're planning a fund-raising event, your local branch of McDonalds will supply free orange juice on a stand manned by a staff member. This can be used either as free refreshment or sold to raise cash. Contact your local branch manager for details and booking.

SOUTH WEST

AIRFARES GUIDE

48 QUEEN ST, EXETER, DEVON EX4 7SR

☎ (01392) 490909. (MAIL ORDER.)

Taking a holiday abroad once you have a family is an expensive business. Find out how to travel without paying the full fare by subscribing to the Airfares Guide. Updated monthly and published quarterly, it lists thousands of cheap air fares for hundreds of destinations, with details of how to buy the tickets. How it works is that consolidators ("wholesalers") approach airlines and offer to bulk buy tickets to particular destinations at favourable prices. The airline only appoints a few consolidators, who then sell on to the travel agent trade, who sell the tickets to you, with appropriate mark-ups along the way. The Airfares Guide enables you to bypass the travel agent and go directly to the consolidator and buy the tickets at "wholesale" prices. Or if you feel uncomfortable with that, you can ask your travel agent to buy from a named consolidator and charge you a handling fee. The Guide lists destinations with one-way and return fairs (including their restrictions) and the seasons they're valid for. Then it lists the code of the agent or consolidator offering that fare, which you can look up in the back of the Guide to find the telephone number and book the ticket yourself. The Guide costs £49.50 a year or £15 a quarter. The company also publishes other publications with money-saving ideas for travellers.

Fire Defence and Brigade's Museum has fire-fighting displays using the early hand pumps, uniforms, helmets and equipment. It's only open one afternoon each month, when entrance is free, but you can make an appointment to see it at other times. The Museum is at Potterne, Devizes, Wiltshire. Phone (01380) 723601.

BABYCARE LTD

113A DORCHESTER ROAD, WEYMOUTH, DORSET
☎ (01305) 788095. OPEN 9.30 – 5.30 MON – SAT,
CLOSED AT 1 ON WEDS.

Toys, baby feeding equipment, premature baby clothes,
nursery equipment including prams, cots and pushchairs from
Mamas & Papas and Silver Cross at prices which are lower than
those in department stores. Babycare advertise the fact that they
will beat anybody else's price. There is also a repair workshop
for the manufacturers they stock: Maclaren, Britax and Bebe
Confort.

CARGO CLUB

CASTLE COURT, BRISTOL, AVON
☎ (0117) 9728811. OPEN 9 – 8 MON – WED, 9 – 9 THUR,
9 – 10 FRI, 8.30 – 7 SAT, 10 – 6 SUN.

A family means bigger food bills and anything that can help
defray the costs is welcome. Cargo Club is a British-owned
warehouse club which is open to members only, but membership is not very restrictive. You have to be either VAT registered
or a member of a certain profession – ring your local outlet for
membership details. There is an enormous range of goods from
brand name foods – Heinz baked beans, Coca Cola, butter,
cheese, toilet paper, breakfast cereals – plus fresh meat, clothes,
games, books, computers, camcorders, bedroom furniture, high
chairs, playpens, toddler's beds and mattresses. All are very
competitively priced indeed, although you may have to buy
packs of four or more of food items.

CHILD'S PLAY

28 ALBION STREET, EXMOUTH, DEVON EX8 1JJ
☎ (01395) 276975. OPEN 10 – 4 MON, TUE, THUR-SAT,
10 – 1 WED, CLOSED 1 – 2 DAILY.

Secondhand and new baby equipment and clothes for ages 0–6
years. Babygros cost from 50p to £2.99; prams from £5 to
£100.

CRAZY MAC'S

FLEET LANE, FLEETBRIDGE, POOLE, DORSET BH15 3BZ
☎ (01202) 666567. OPEN SEVEN DAYS A WEEK.
Enormous, 62,000 sq ft outlet selling liquidated, salvage and
clearance stock from furniture to electrical goods. There is a
children's clothing department and the outlet also sells toys,
bunk beds, cots, prams and, depending on what comes in, a
variety of other child-oriented merchandise.

ROUNDABOUT

2 PRIOR PARK ROAD, WIDCOMBE, BATH, AVON
☎ (01225) 316696. OPEN 9.30 – 5 MON – SAT.
Great savings on secondhand cots, playpens, prams and baby
alarms. Limited parking near the shop, but there is a car park
across the road.

THE BISCUIT BAKERY

MOORES BISCUITS, MORCOMBELAKE, NR BRIDPORT, DORSET
DT6 6ES
☎ (01297) 89253. OPEN 9 – 5 MON – FRI, 9 – 1 SAT FROM
MAY TO SEPT.
Broken biscuits including shortbreads, walnut crunch, chocolate chip and ginger biscuits sold in 800 gram bags at 30%
saving. Tend to sell out very early in the day, so don't leave your
visit until late in the afternoon.

The Donkey Sanctuary near Sidmouth, Devon, is home to more than 400
retired or ill-treated donkeys. Many are former beach donkeys, others are
victims of cruelty. There are guided tours of the donkey sanctuary with case
histories of some of the incumbents, and visitors are free to roam at will
and stroke the donkeys. There is no entrance charge. The Sanctuary is
located on the A3052 Exeter to Lyme Regis road, near Sitford. Phone 01395
516391.

WALES AND WEST MIDLANDS

BOOKS FOR CHILDREN

MEMBERSHIP SERVICES DEPARTMENT, PO BOX 70,
CIRENCESTER, GLOS GL7 7AZ
☎ 0181-606 3030. MAIL ORDER.

Free membership to individuals, though you have to order four books in the first year. Caters for under fives to over tens. The colour magazine publishes the usual publisher's price and the discounted club price. Publishers include Dorling Kindersley, Hodder & Stoughton, Heinemann, Hamlyn and Oxford University Press.

CADBURY WORLD

PO BOX 1958, LINDEN ROAD, BOURNEVILLE, BIRMINGHAM,
WEST MIDLANDS B30 2LD
☎ (0121) 451 4159. OPENING TIMES VARY, PHONE (0121) 451 4180 FOR OPENING TIMES AND TICKET PRICES.

See the history of chocolate from the Aztec days to modern production methods and visit the souvenir gift shop at the end. The shop has a bargain corner where misshapes, cancelled orders or close to date code items from the famous Cadbury's chocolate range sells at discount prices. Most of the products sold in the retail shop are prime stock and therefore charged appropriately, but a maximum of ten lines at any one time of stock which cannot be supplied to Cadbury's retail customers, is sold in the shop. There's also a restaurant, baby changing facilities and a children's play area.

CARGO CLUB

AXLETREE WAY, WEDNESBURY, WEST MIDLANDS
WS10 9QY
☎ (0121) 568 8668. OPEN 10 – 8 MON – WED,
10 – 9 THUR, FRI, 9 – 7 SAT, 10 – 6 SUN.

A family means bigger food bills and anything that can help

defray the costs is welcome. Cargo Club is a British-owned warehouse club which is open to members only, but membership is not very restrictive. You have to be either VAT registered or a member of a certain profession – ring your local outlet for membership details. There is an enormous range of goods from brand name foods – Heinz baked beans, Coca Cola, butter, cheese, toilet paper, breakfast cereals – plus fresh meat, clothes, games, books, computers, camcorders, bedroom furniture, high chairs, playpens, toddler's beds and mattresses. All are very competitively priced indeed, although you may have to buy packs of four or more of food items.

HAWK CYCLES LIQUIDATIONS

FORGE LANE, CRADLEY HEATH, WEST MIDLANDS B64 5AL
☎ (01384) 636535. OPEN 9 – 8 MON – SAT, 9 – 4.30 SUN.
Sells all types of childrens' bikes, as well as adult ones, direct to the public at factory prices. Children's trikes start at £10.99, adult mountain bikes at £89.99.

LILLIPUT AND JACK IN THE BOX

63 AVON CRESCENT, STRATFORD-UPON-AVON, WARWICKSHIRE
☎ (01789) 267991. OPEN 10 – 4 TUE – SAT.
Children's toys, secondhand clothes and baby equipment from 0–10 years.

LITTLE GEMS

20 COTEN END, WARWICKSHIRE CV34 4NP
☎ (01926) 408248. OPEN 10 – 5 MON – FRI,
10.30 – 4 SAT.
Secondhand equipment ranges from high chairs and playpens to prams, buggies and Moses baskets, usually at less than half the normal retail price. There are also secondhand toys from Fisher-Price to Matchbox, as well as sterilisers, breast pumps, stair gates, fire guards, cots, sleeping bags, bed linen and cot linen, matinee jackets and shawls. At time of going to press, they were planning to offer a hire service, too.

NIPPERS

FIELDS FARM, MARTON, NEAR RUGBY, WARWICKSHIRE
CV23 9RS
☎ (01926) 633100. (01926) 633007. OPENING HOURS
VARY SO PHONE FIRST.
ORCHARD COTTAGE FARM, CROOME ROAD, DEFFORD,
WORCESTER WR8 9AS
☎ (01386) 750888. (01386) 750333 FAX. OPENING HOURS
VARY SO PHONE FIRST.

Nippers, the nursery equipment and toy specialists, started with a very clever and simple idea and have now built it up to create an award-winning chain of franchises. The company operates from converted barns on farms around the country, offering easy parking, no queues, and personal service. This is on top of competitive prices on prams, cots, pushchairs, car seats, outdoor play equipment and toys. Prices are low partly because they operate from farms, with none of the overheads of traditional retail outlets, and party because the successful growth of a number of branches means it can now buy in bulk and negotiate good deals. Customers can try out the merchandise and the children can see the animals, mostly sheep and pigs. Familiar brand names are on sale at all the branches, including Britax and Bebe Confort, Fisher-Price and Little Tikes. You can try out the car seats in your car and there is usually a pram/pushchair repair service on site.

Museum of Science and Industry in Birmingham is on three levels with an aircraft section featuring a Spitfire and a Hurricane; a fire arms section with guns on display, as well as locomotives and trams; and a large engineering hall with a science section with computers and toys. There are lots of hands-on activities and entrance is free. The Museum is at Newhall Street, Birmingham. Phone (0121) 235 1661.

PRAMS DIRECT

UNIT 1, KELVIN WAY, WEST BROMWICH, WEST MIDLANDS
B70 7JW
☎ (0121) 525 5162. OPEN 9 – 5 MON – FRI.
The mail order arm of a shop called Nursery to Leisure, Prams
Direct does stock reconditioned Maclaren prams and pushchairs as well as factory seconds. Its main advantage, though, is
that it allows new parents to choose the piece of equipment they
want and have it delivered to their door. They will send you
catalogues of any of the manufacturers of your choice and you
can then ring Prams Direct to order.

SCHOLASTIC BOOK CLUBS

WESTFIELD HOUSE, SOUTHAM, LEAMINGTON SPA,
WARWICKSHIRE CV33 0JH
☎ (01926) 813910. MAIL ORDER.
Aimed at schools, they will send packs to groups at a nursery or
playschool. There is no minimum number for a group. There
are four clubs aimed at different age ranges from pre-school to
ten plus, each with their own newsletter with about 30 books in
each. Books are sold at discount prices and organisers get a 10%
discount or one free book for every ten purchased.

THE BOOKSHOP

THE PAVEMENT, HAY ON WYE HR3 5BU
☎ (01497) 821341. OPEN 9 – 8 MON – SUN.
Secondhand and remaindered books, as well as new and review
copies, are sold in this huge shop, including recently published
books, usually one-third off and sometimes half price.

THE RED HOUSE

RANGE ROAD, COTSWOLD BUSINESS PARK, WITNEY,
OXFORDSHIRE OX8 5YF
☎ (01993) 771144. MAIL ORDER.
An excellent catalogue of children's books, The Red House
covers both educational matters, from learning to read to
history, and practical activity books as well as fiction. The books

are a mixture of hardback and paperback and good savings are to be made. The Red House also runs a Birthday Club where you can buy everything you need for a children's party – apart from the food.

THE SWAN FACTORY SHOP

POPE STREET, HOCKLEY, BIRMINGHAM B1 3DL

☎ (0121) 200 1313. OPEN 9 – 4 MON – FRI, 9 – 1 SAT.

Mixing up baby food or making some interesting, home made soups for the family is easier with the right equipment. Moulinex, Swan and Krupps kitchen appliances as well as microwaves, kettles, toasters, electric knives, irons, saucepans and frying pans are on sale here. All are seconds or discontinued items with some slightly imperfect but electrically sound. A top of the range food processor which would cost £150 in department stores would sell for £100 here.

TP ACTIVITY TOYS FACTORY SHOP

SEVERN ROAD, STOURPORT-ON-SEVERN, WORCESTER, WORCESTERSHIRE DY13 9EX

☎ (01299) 827728. 9 – 5 MON – FRI, 9.30 – 4.30 SAT.

A full range of outdoor and indoor play equipment from swings and climbing frames to sand trays and tree houses, some of which are discounted at certain times of the year as they are used as display items and aren't as pristine. There is usually one big factory site sale every year as well, which is well worth going to. Site shop has Galt, Tomy and masses of toys and games, but not at discounted prices.

For ideas about places to visit on family outings, visit your local tourist board or tourist information office where there are usually scores of leaflets and booklets about your area. They are often useful education tools, too, as they offer historical and geographical information which you can pass onto your children on the spot.

EAST ANGLIA AND EAST MIDLANDS

CASTAWAYS

10 BURTON ROAD, LINCOLN LN1 3LB

☎ (01522) 546035. OPEN 9.30 – 4.30 MON – SAT,
CLOSED WEDS.

An agency shop specialising in almost new children's clothing,
nursery equipment, toys and ladies' fashions and accessories.
Smart mums-to-be know this is the place to go to find not only a
complete wardrobe but also the layette. Only items that look
virtually new and are fashionable are selected for sale.

EDWARDIAN CONFECTIONERY LTD

HUTHWAITE, BARKER STREET, SUTTON IN ASHFIELD,
NOTTINGHAMSHIRE NG17 2LG

☎ (01623) 554712. OPEN 9 – 6 MON – FRI,
9.30 – 12.30 SAT.

Sweets and rock made on the premises and sold at two-thirds of
the shop price. Range includes rock and boiled sweets, peanut
brittle, treacle slab, caramel slab and chocolate, peanut and
raisin slab, all of which can be bought either whole or broken
up.

GALLOWAY & PORTER

THE PADDOCKS, CHERRYHINTON ROAD,
CAMBRIDGE CB1 4DH

☎ (01223) 67876.

Holds regular book warehouse sales about once a month on a
Saturday from 9–5 at which most books cost £1 or £2, regardless
of the original price. Children's books tend to be for the under
sevens and cost £1 each. Free parking. There is a shop at 30
Sidney Street, Cambridge which is open six days a week from
8.30–5.30 which also sells good value books.

GILCHRIST CONFECTIONERY LTD

UNITS 1 & 2, OXBOROUGH LANE, FAKENHAM,
NORFOLK NR21 8AF
☎ (01328) 862632. OPEN 8 – 3 THUR.
Factory shop underneath the offices sells all sorts of chocolate
items – walnut whips, petit fours, mints, Thomas the Tank
Engine chololates, Christmas chocolate tree decorations – to
well known department stores. Seconds and misshapes are sold
at discount in bags. Stock varies from week to week.

NIPPERS

HALL FARM, FLAWBOROUGH, NOTTINGHAM NG13 9PA
☎ (01949) 51244. (01949) 51335 FAX. OPENING HOURS
VARY SO PHONE FIRST.
THE MANOR, TUR LANGTON, LEICESTER LE8 0PJ
(01858) 545434. (01858) 545774 FAX.
Nippers, the nursery equipment and toy specialists, started with
a very clever and simple idea and have now built it up to create
an award-winning chain of franchises. The company operates
from converted barns on farms around the country, offering
easy parking, no queues, and personal service. This is on top of
competitive prices on prams, cots, pushchairs, car seats,
outdoor play equipment and toys. Prices are low partly because
they operate from farms, with none of the overheads of
traditional retail outlets, and party because the successful
growth of a number of branches means it can now buy in bulk
and negotiate good deals. Customers can try out the merchandise and the children can see the animals, mostly sheep and
pigs. Familiar brand names are on sale at all the branches,
including Britax and Bebe Confort, Fisher-Price and Little Tikes.
You can try out the car seats in your car and there is usually a
pram/pushchair repair service on site.

Put the cot diagonally across the room (on a corner) to make it easier to
get round to make up the cot.

STAGE 2

SAVILLE ROAD, WESTWOOD, PETERBOROUGH,
CAMBRIDGESHIRE PE3 7PR
☎ (01733) 263308. OPEN 10 – 8 MON – FRI,
9 – 6 SAT AND BANK HOLIDAYS.
THE RIVERSIDE RETAIL PARK, QUEEN'S DRIVE,
NOTTINGHAM NG2 1RU
☎ (0115) 9865812. OPEN 10 – 8 MON – FRI, 9 – 6 SAT,
11 – 5 SUN AND BANK HOLIDAYS.
UNIT 3, TRITTON RETAIL PARK, CENTURION ROAD,
LINCOLN LN1
☎ (01522) 560303. OPEN 10 – 8 MON – FRI, 9 – 6 SAT,
10 – 4 BANK HOLIDAYS.

These are Freeman's mail order discount stores which sell
discontinued lines, soiled and returned goods from the full
range as seen in the catalogue at discount prices. There are
children's clothes from underwear to raincoats, toys, and
nursery equipment at 50% of the full catalogue price. There is
also a British shoe concession in the Peterborough store which
also sells at discount.

THE BOOKWORM CLUB

HEFFERS BOOKSELLERS, 20 TRINITY STREET, CAMBRIDGE,
CAMBRIDGESHIRE CB2 3NG
☎ (01223) 568568.

Free to teachers, groups of parents or PTA members, but not for
individuals. Children choose from two leaflets aimed at two to
16 year olds. Books are sold at the full published price, but 10%
of the value of the total order is refunded to the organiser.
Moreover, there is an introductory offer which can be ten free
books.

If you have to remove a splinter from a child's finger, it is a good idea to
rub the spot with an ice cube first. The cold will act as an anaesthetic and
reduce the pain.

THE UPPINGHAM DRESS AGENCY

2-6 ORANGE STREET, UPPINGHAM, RUTLAND LE15 9SQ
☎ (01572) 823276. OPEN 9 – 5.30 MON – SAT,
12 – 4 SUN AND BANK HOLIDAYS.

One of the oldest and possibly the largest dress agency in the country with 12 rooms on three floors packed with quality nearly-new clothing for children, men and women. One room on the first floor is devoted to children, although there are also children's sizes in the room with riding clothes and hacking jackets. Buggies can be left on the ground floor where there is a lounge with free coffee.

THORNTONS

38 KING STREET BELPER, DERBYSHIRE DE5 1PL
☎ (01773) 827222. OPEN 9 – 5.30 MON – SAT.

Although the factory shop has now closed, Thorntons shop in the nearby high street has a "quality clearance" corner which sells, as well as lollipops and bars, mis-shapes. Some of the good deals on offer include half-price Continental chocolates, Thorntons luxury selection and half-pound pack bars. Visit it on a Thursday, as they re-stock on a Wednesday.

WILLOW TRADING

WILLOWS TRADING ESTATE, FINBOROUGH ROAD,
STOWMARKET, SUFFOLK IP14 3BU
☎ (01499) 771261. OPEN 10 – 5.30 THUR – SAT.

A catalogue shop which sells catalogue returns from the Freeman's mail order brochure. This can include anything the catalogue sells, but stock varies so it is best to ring before visiting. There are children's clothes from the Clothkits range, as well as nursery equipment such as prams, pushchairs, and cots.

NORTH WEST, YORKSHIRE AND HUMBERSIDE

B LEWIS & SONS LTD

FACTORY SHOP, MIDDLEGATE, WHITE LUND INDUSTRIAL
ESTATE, MORECAMBE, LANCASHIRE LA3 3BN
☎ (01524) 61616. OPEN 9 – 5 MON – FRI, 9 – 12 SAT,
SUN IN SUMMER, SAT ONLY IN WINTER.
Ice creams, gâteaux and frozen foods from Norpark, Homefarm
and Bird's Eye which are sold at prices lower than in the shops.
Own brand ice cream sells at 30–40p less on the 2-litre quantity,
and Black Forest Gâteau costs about £2 less than in the shops.
You do not have to bulk buy, but orders are only delivered
(locally only) if the total is more than £30.

EVERYTHING BUT THE BABY

19 KNARESBOROUGH ROAD, HARROGATE,
YORKSHIRE HG2 7SR
☎ (01423) 888292. OPEN 10 – 4 MON – SAT,
CLOSED 1 WED.
Nearly-new shop selling expansive range of babywear and
baby equipment up to the age of five. Pushchairs and car seats,
all fully checked, and clothes range from Marks & Spencer and
Ladybird to OshKosh and Oilily.

KIPPAX BISCUITS LTD

FACTORY SHOP, KING STREET, COLNE,
LANCASHIRE BB8 9HU
☎ (01282) 864 198. OPEN 10 – 3.45 WED, FRI, SAT,
CLOSED 1 – 1.15.
More than 100 different types of biscuits from ginger wafers and
shortbread to plain assorted and chocolate sold in packets, tins
or loose. The top 15 products sell at 90p per pound, while
misshapes cost 60p per pound with chocolate misshapes

costing £1 per pound. Tins and boxes of biscuits from £1.75–£5.

MR BABY

4 ST JOHN'S ROAD, HUDDERSFIELD, YORKSHIRE
☎ (01484) 515381. OPEN 9 – 5.30 MON – SAT.

Sells reconditioned, seconds and former showroom models of the Mamas & Papas range, as well as full-price infant clothes and nursery equipment from other manufacturers. It sometimes has discounted pram samples from Maclaren and Silver Cross, as well as everything for the nursery. Infant clothes include Baby-Mini and Petit Bateau.

NIPPERS

RECTORY FARM, MIDDLE STREET, NAFFERTON, DRIFFIELD, EAST YORKSHIRE YO25 0JS
☎ (01377) 240689. (01377) 240687 FAX. OPEN 10 – 4 MON – FRI, 10 – 5 SAT, 2 – 4 SUN.

Nippers, the nursery equipment and toy specialists, started with a very clever and simple idea and have now built it up to create an award-winning chain of franchises. The company operates from converted barns on farms around the country, offering easy parking, no queues, and personal service. This is on top of competitive prices on prams, cots, pushchairs, car seats, outdoor play equipment and toys. Prices are low partly because they operate from farms, with none of the overheads of traditional retail outlets, and party because the successful growth of a number of branches means it can now buy in bulk and negotiate good deals. Customers can try out the merchandise and the children can see the animals, mostly sheep and pigs. Familiar brand names are on sale at all the branches, including Britax and Bebe Confort, Fisher-Price and Little Tikes. You can try out the car seats in your car and there is usually a pram/pushchair repair service on site.

THE BUBBLE FACTORY

MOSCOW MILL, COLLIER STREET, OSWALD TWISTLE,
NR ACCRINGTON, LANCASHIRE BB5 3DF
☎ (01254) 871025. OPEN 9 – 5 MON – SAT, 10 – 5 SUN.
Keep the germs at bay when baby is crawling. This factory shop
sells everything you need to keep the house clean, including
brand-names such as JIF, Comfort and Flash. And you don't
have to bulk buy. There is also a separate shop in the complex
selling textiles, including bedding and towels, at factory prices.

THORNTON'S

ST JOHN'S SHOPPING CENTRE, LANCASTER WAY, PRESTON,
LANCASHIRE
☎ (01772) 202421. OPEN 9 – 5.30 MON – SAT.
Sells misshapes at bargain prices. Continental misshapes cost
£1.49 for a half pound, Select misshapes cost £1.69 a half
pound. Also specific children's lines from time to time.

BEBE CONFORT
☎ (01732) 740880.

As a manufacturer, Bebe Confort does not sell direct to the public, but it
does supply some shops with ends of lines. Finding these shops can be a
time-consuming business. First, phone head office on the telephone
number given above and ask for the names of your local stockists. You
then have to phone round the stockists and ask if they have any end of
season lines or discontinued ranges.

NORTH AND SCOTLAND

NORTHUMBRIAN FINE FOOD PLC

DUKES WAY, TEAM VALLEY INDUSTRIAL ESTATE,
TYNE & WEAR NE11 0QP
☎ (0191) 482 2611. OPEN 9.30 – 1.30 MON – FRI.
As a leading manufacturer of biscuits and cakes, Northumbrian
Fine Foods sell standard products and over-runs through their
factory outlet. Product availability changes, depending upon
production but typically there are plain and chocolate biscuits,
flap jacks, cakes, cookies and confectionery on sale. Brand
names include Dunkers, Sunwheel, Prewetts and Country
Fitness Foods.

SHARK SPORTS

NORDSTROM HOUSE, NORTH BROOMHILL, MORPETH,
NEAR AMBLER, NORTHUMBERLAND NE65 9UJ
☎ (01670) 760365. OPEN 9.30 – 4.30 MON – FRI,
9.30 – 12 SAT.
Manufactures and sells in the factory shop wetsuits, dry suits,
diving suits, buoyancy aids, diving boots, and gloves for
children from two years of age, as well as for men and women,
at factory prices. Also sells the occasional mask and some fins.
Children's one-piece wetsuits, £37.50–£40; also sells two-piece
wetsuits.

SHAW'S DUNDEE SWEET FACTORY

FULTON ROAD, WESTER GOURDIE INDUSTRIAL ESTATE,
DUNDEE DD2 4SW
☎ (01382) 610369. OPEN 11.30 – 4 MON – FRI IN
SUMMER, 1.30 – 4 IN WINTER.
Specialises in fudge and boiled sweets, tablet and tray toffee.
Discounts and special offers always available.

TURNABOUT

32 PRIORY PLACE, CRAIGIE, PERTH, SCOTLAND
☎ (01738) 630916. OPEN 9.30 – 5 MON – FRI, 10 – 4 SAT.
Nearly-new children's clothes from birth to ten years, as well as equipment from high chairs, cots, prams and buggies to playpens and car seats. They also hire out baby equipment and at time of going to press were planning to sell new children's clothes made on the premises.

Planning a fund-raising event which will involve children? They love bouncy castles, but they're expensive to hire. Contact the country's leading building society, The Halifax, who will supply bouncy castles and the staff to man them for charitable events, as long as there are 1,000 people attending. Apply in writing to your local branch for details well in advance of the event as they tend to be very booked up.

CHRISTENING AND BIRTHDAY GIFTS

LONDON

DAVID RICHARDS & SONS

12 NEW CAVENDISH STREET, LONDON W1M 7LJ

☎ 0171-935 3206. OPEN 9.30 – 5.30 MON – FRI.

Silver photograph frames, silver baby rattles, silver children's mugs, silver napkin rings, silver spoons, silver dummies, silver clocks, silver baby brush and comb sets. Twenty-four hour engraving service. Service is well informed and courteous, and prices are much more reasonable than comparable prices in the high street. This is due to the fact that because the shop wholesales in Britain and Europe, it buys enormous quantities and is thus able to pass on bulk-buying savings to customers.

ROBERTS AND DORE LTD

31-35 KIRBY STREET, HATTON GARDEN,
LONDON EC1N 8TE

☎ 0171-405 1114. OPEN 9 – 5 MON – FRI.

Established in 1908, this family business are independent manufacturing silversmiths and cutlers who supply department stores and specialist shops throughout the world. They make a wide selection of products suitable for christening and birthday presents including napkin rings, pewter mugs, small photograph frames, most of which can be engraved. All prices are based on half the recommended retail selling price. There are also some special sale offers available at this trade showroom and warehouse at certain times of year, which are normally invitation only. Repairs and replating are undertaken.

THE SALVAGE SHOP

34-36 WATLING AVENUE, BURNT OAK,
MIDDLESEX HA8 0LR

☎ 0181-952 4353. OPEN 9 – 5 MON – SAT.

An Aladdin's cave of "salvaged" stock for the avid bargain hunter, most of which has been the subject of bankruptcy, insurance claims, fire or flood. There is often a small selection of electrical equipment for older children and toys often with damaged packaging, but the widest selection is for adults. Discounts range from 50%–75%. Phone first to check stock.

Some museums offer free entrance after a certain time of day, usually an hour or two before closing. The Imperial War Museum in Lambeth Road, London, for instance, is free after 4.30pm on weekdays and weekends, leaving you one and a half hours to enjoy the exhibitions. Check out your local museums.

SOUTH EAST

HEIRLOOMS LTD
2 ARUN BUSINESS PARK, BOGNOR REGIS,
WEST SUSSEX PO22 9SX
☎ (01243) 820252. OPEN ONCE A MONTH,
USUALLY 10 – 5 ON THE FIRST FRIDAY AND SOME SUNS
AND BANK HOLIDAYS. PHONE FIRST FOR A LIST OF OPEN
DAY DATES.
Traditional christening robes and baby clothes up to the age of
six, hand-embroidered with lace, and perfect for weddings and
parties. Silver and gold plated teddy bear picture frames,
napkin rings and other christening gifts, plus nursery bed
linens. Prices are anything from 18%–60% off the recommended retail price for slight seconds or perfect merchandise since
you are buying directly from the manufacturer.

LOUIS POTTS & CO
43 CLIFFE HIGH STREET, LEWES, EAST SUSSEX BN7 2AN
☎ (01273) 472240. OPEN 9.30 – 5.30 MON – SAT.
China and glass from Wedgwood, Royal Doulton and Denby,
among others, at prices between 5% and 25% below those in
large department stores. Includes Peter Pan designs on
Wedgwood, Mad Hatters on Poole and Bramley Hedge and
Bunnykins on Royal Doulton, as well as cartoon mugs.

NAZEING GLASS
NAZEING NEW ROAD, BROXBOURNE, ESSEX EM10 6SU
☎ (01992) 464485. OPEN 9.30 – 4.30 MON – FRI,
9.30 – 3 SAT.
A factory shop selling cut glass, many of which are suitable for
christening presents – glass slippers, tankards, glass bells – the
latter two of which can be engraved. Factory shop prices in
practice mean at least 20% off.

SOUTH WEST

DARTINGTON CRYSTAL
SCHOOL LANE, TORRINGTON, DEVON EX38 7AN
☎ (01805) 622321. OPEN 9.30 – 5 MON – SAT.
A factory shop selling an across-the-board selection of Dartington crystal seconds at 20%–30% discounts, as well as some perfects at full price. Tankards, goblets and bowls are bought regularly as christening gifts, and engraved on the premises.

DARTMOUTH POTTERY
WARFLEET, DARTMOUTH, DEVON TQ6 9BY
☎ (01803) 832258. OPEN 10 – 5 MON – SAT.
Discontinued lines and some perfects of Dartmouth pottery at varied discounts. Always some special offers on; prices range from 50p to £15. Small range of mugs, egg cups, cereal bowls, plates, toast racks and honey pots with teddy bear design.

DOWNTON TRADING COMPANY
THE OLD MANSION HOUSE, NO 3 THE HIGH STREET,
DOWNTON, NR SALISBURY, WILTSHIRE SP5 3PG
☎ (01725) 510676. OPEN 9.30 – 5 MON – SAT.
Unique shop which sells more than three dozen other top companies' seconds, ends of lines and clearance items at reduced prices. Many of the companies whose merchandise is on sale here can be found in the top gift stores. There are items suitable for gifts for children such as nursery bags in designer fabrics, pretty lamps and lampshades, some superb silver and pewter items, limited edition prints, rugby shirts, photograph frames, headbands, floppy teddies and bunnies and hand bound photograph albums. Everything is marked with a coloured label which denotes whether it is a slight second, discounted item, the result of over-production or an end of line. Stock will change on a three-monthly basis so you may find different, but just as high quality, items in the shop when you visit.

WALES AND WEST MIDLANDS

ISIS CERAMICS

THE OLD TOFFEE FACTORY, 120A MARLBOROUGH ROAD,
OXFORD, OXFORDSHIRE OX1 4LS
☎ (01865) 722729. OPEN 10 – 4 MON – FRI.
Good range of animal delftware seconds, which would make
good christening presents, on sale at the workshop. Also do
inscribed plates, but only at full price.

MINTON BONE CHINA & ROYAL DOULTON

MINTON HOUSE, LONDON ROAD, STOKE-ON-TRENT,
STAFFORDSHIRE ST4 7QD
☎ (01782) 229292. OPEN 9 – 5.30 MON – SAT.
Best quality Royal Crown Derby and Royal Doulton Crystal at
promotion prices. Bramley Hedge, Beatrix Potter, Bunnykins
figures and assorted tableware, all at reduced prices.

MOORLAND POTTERY

CHELSEA WORKS, 72A MOORLAND ROAD, BURSLEM,
STAFFORDSHIRE ST6 1DY
☎ (01782) 834631. OPEN 9 – 5 MON – FRI.
Baby mugs, from £3.75, pigs, geese, frogs plus plates, bowls and
mugs with various designs. Prices are very competitive.

ROYAL BRIERLEY CRYSTAL

BRIERLEY HILL, WEST MIDLANDS
☎ (01384) 573580. OPEN 9.30 – 5.30 MON – FRI,
9 – 5 SAT, 10 – 4 SUN.
Sells seconds of Royal Brierley crystal at 30%–40% discount as
well as a selection of Royal Worcester. Customers usually
choose Royal Brierley tankards or goblets as christening
presents and have them engraved on the premises.

ROYAL DOULTON

NILE STREET, BURSLEM, STAFFORDSHIRE

☎ (01782) 292292. OPEN 9 – 5.30 MON – SAT.

Factory shop selling seconds and overmakes of the Royal Doulton range. Christening sets available in Bunnykins designs, also plates, mugs, moneyballs and Beatrix Potter figures, Also a museum and showroom. Tours are available, though they are more suitable for older children.

ROYAL GRAFTON CHINA

MARLBOROUGH ROAD, LONGTON, STOKE-ON-TRENT,
STAFFORDSHIRE ST3 1ED

☎ (01782) 599667. OPEN 9 – 4.30 MON – FRI, 9 – 3 SAT.

Discounted prices for seconds and discontinued lines. Factory shop has discounts of up to 75% off chinaware. There are christening sets, money boxes, plates, bowls, two-handled and one-handled mugs and egg cups.

SPODE LTD

CHURCH STREET, STOKE-ON-TRENT,
STAFFORDSHIRE ST4 1BX

☎ (01782) 744011. OPEN 9 – 5 MON – SAT.

Factory shop selling Spode china, including blue and white figures from Edwardian childhood which make good christening presents, as well as cereal bowls, egg plates and mugs, all seconds and at discounts of about 35%. There are regular sales at which discounts of 75% are available on some discontinued lines. There's also a museum and factory tours can be arranged.

Museum of Science and Industry in Birmingham is on three levels with an aircraft section featuring a Spitfire and a Hurricane; a fire arms section with guns on display, as well as locomotives and trams; and a large engineering hall with a science section with computers and toys. There are lots of hands-on activities and entrance is free. The Museum is at Newhall Street, Birmingham. Phone (0121) 235 1661.

WEDGWOOD

LICHFIELD STREET, HANLEY, STOKE-ON-TRENT,
STAFFORDSHIRE ST1 3EJ
☎ (01782) 263934. OPEN 9 – 5 MON – SAT, 10 – 4 SUN.
Seconds are sold at the normal retail price minus 40%. There's a
nursery range of Wedgwood Peter Rabbit, Thomas the Tank
Engine and Rupert Bear wall clocks, £15.95 usual price about
£27, plus Coalport figurines, jugs, vases. There's also a
museum, craft demonstration area, cinema and refreshment
lounge at the Barlaston site.

Most new mothers receive a Bounty Pack when they are in hospital after
giving birth. This contains samples and sometimes even full-size packs of a
wide range of products from baby lotion, wipes and shampoo to nappy
sacks, toothpaste, nappies and photographic discounts. It's useful for trying
out products before deciding whether they suit you and your baby. The new
mother pack also contains a Babycare book which has a claim card which
you can redeem at Boots the Chemist for a Baby Progress Pack when your
child is four months. This gives you products appropriate to your baby's
age such as baby food, drink, rusks, powdered meals, etc. The mothers of
more than 800,000 babies a year receive these packs.

EAST ANGLIA AND EAST MIDLANDS

CAITHNESS CRYSTAL

HARDWICK INDUSTRIAL ESTATE, KINGS LYNN,
NORFOLK NR25 7DG
☎ (01553) 765111. OPEN 9 – 5 MON – SAT,
11 – 4.30 SUN AT EASTER AND CHRISTMAS ONLY.
Tankards which can be engraved with child's name on the premises.

MRS PICKERING'S DOLLS' CLOTHES

THE PINES, DECOY ROAD, POTTER HEIGHAM,
GREAT YARMOUTH, NORFOLK NR29 5LX
☎ (01692) 670407. OPEN 8 – 8 MON – FRI. MAIL ORDER
WITH SAE ONLY.
Dolls' clothes made for any doll which, Mrs Pickering claims, won't fall apart straight away, are easy to put on and take off, and, especially for smaller children, will help them to learn to use various methods of fastenings. All the popular dolls are catered for – including Tiny Tears, Timmy, Action Man, Sindy, My First Tiny Tears, Fisher-Price Babies, teddy bears, trolls and Cabbage Patch Babies – and special outfits can be made on request.

ROYAL CROWN DERBY

194 OSMASTON ROAD, DERBY, DERBYSHIRE DE23 8JZ
☎ (01332) 712835. OPEN 9 – 5 MON – SAT.
One third of the stock is made up of seconds of bone china at discount prices. Occasionally have christening mugs as seconds.

STANDARD SOAP COMPANY LTD

DERBY RD, ASHBY-DE-LA-ZOUCH, LEICESTERSHIRE
LE65 2HG
☎ (01530) 414281. OPEN 10.30 – 5.30 MON, 9.30 – 5.30
TUE – THUR, 9.30 – 3 FRI.

Manufacturers to brand name retailers, they have a small factory shop selling seconds and ends of lines of well known soaps. You buy a basket for 99p and fill them with products from a range which includes soap (10 for £1.50), shampoo, foam bath, talcum powder (35p) face cloths.

You can get a free 128-page pregnancy guide called *Emma's Diary* from your GP as soon as your pregnancy is confirmed. Published for the Royal College of General Practitioners by Lifecycle Marketing, *Emma's Diary* takes you through pregnancy; with helpful advice and includes a claim card for a free gift pack from branches of Boots or Children's World. Your GP or midwife can get free supplies of *Emma's Diary* by writing to RCGP, *Emma's Diary*, Freepost (No SL1 313), Maidenhead, Berks SL6 7YA, or by phoning 01628 771232. Copies can only be supplied to registered GP surgery addresses.

NORTH WEST, YORKSHIRE AND HUMBERSIDE

THE DAVID MELLOR FACTORY SHOP

THE ROUND BUILDING, HATHERSAGE, SHEFFIELD S30 1BA
☎ (01433) 650220. OPEN 10 – 5 MON – SAT, 11 – 5 SUN.
David Mellor's classic cutlery at discounts of 15%, including the
children's range, made from high-grade stainless steel scaled
down in size, which comes in boxed sets of three: a yellow fork,
blue knife and red spoon. The usual price is £15.95, but it's on
sale here for £13.56. The shop is in a former industrial
workshop at an old gasworks in the Peak District.

School project material can be found free if you know where to look. If your
child is studying tea producing areas or nutrition you can get free leaflets
from the Tea Council and many of the supermarkets and manufacturers.
Contact the Tea Council for colourful posters telling where tea comes from
and how it is harvested on 0171-248 1024. Sainsbury's supermarket has a
freephone student line on 0800 387504. Tesco runs a Careline on 0800
505555. John West Foods Ltd sends out information packs – write to the
Marketing Department at West House, Bixteth Street, Liverpool L3 9SR or
phone (0151) 236 8771.

NORTH AND SCOTLAND

HIGHLAND CHINA LTD
OLD STATION YARD, KINGUSSIE, INVERNAYRESSHIRE
PH21 1HP
☎ (01540) 661576. OPEN 9 – 5 MON – FRI.
Bone china and porcelain at up to 50% off. Named mugs, gift
packs, animal designs.

JACKSONS LANDING
THE HIGHLIGHT, HARTLEPOOL MARINA, HARTLEPOOL,
DURHAM TS24 0XN
☎ (01429) 866989. OPEN 10 – 6 MON – SAT, 11 – 5 SUN
AND BANK HOLIDAYS.
Factory shopping village which caters mostly for adults but
does have some factory outlets selling merchandise for children
at discounted prices including JoKids childrenswear and Toy
World which sells Tomy, Fisher-Price and Lego. Some of the
other shops such as Clinkards shoes do sell children's sizes, and
Tog 24 has some small thermal wear and waterproofs. Children
might also be tempted by the Sweet Temptations confectionery.

SECOND CHANCE
27 ALL HALLOWS LANE, KENDAL, CUMBRIA LA9 4JH
☎ (01539) 740414. OPEN 9 – 5.30 MON – SAT.
Sells mostly good quality seconds in English bone china, but
does have a range of mugs and plates with nursery rhyme
themes.

NORTHERN IRELAND

TYRONE CRYSTAL LTD
6-7 BACK ROW, OFF MILL ROAD, DOIGH, BALLYCLARE,
COUNTY ANTRIM
OPEN 10 – 4.30 MON – SAT.
KILLYBRACKEY, DUNGANNON, COUNTY TYRONE BT71 6BN
☎ (01665) 510027. OPEN 9 – 5 MON – SAT.
Factory shop selling first and second quality Tyrone crystal,
although only the second quality products are cheaper at about
one third of the normal price. Stocks christening cups which are
sandblasted with a stork design and can be engraved, also little
bells which can be engraved.

BOOTS THE CHEMIST
BRANCHES COUNTRYWIDE.
☎ (0800) 622 525.

Any parent who's staggered home with the weekly shopping and the
nappies will jump at the chance to have them delivered free. Boots the
Chemist will transport nappies to your home as long as you buy one
month's supply. You can either order and pay at your local store or phone
the free nappy home delivery service number above.

WHEN TO HIRE
RATHER THAN BUY

LONDON

BABY AWAY NURSERY HIRE
56A DOLLIS PARK, FINCHLEY, LONDON NZ 1BS
☎ 0181-343 3552. PHONE FIRST.

KIDDYHIRE
32 GRANGE GARDENS, PINNER, MIDDLESEX HA5 5QE
☎ 0181-868 4368. PHONE FIRST.
33 CHESTNUT AVENUE, PINNER, MIDDLESEX HA5 1LX
☎ 0181-866 5488. PHONE FIRST.

THE NAPPY EXPRESS
128 HIGH ROAD, SOUTHGATE, LONDON N11 1PG
☎ 0181-361 4040. PHONE FIRST.

NURSERY HIRE CO
24 WHITEHALL GARDENS, LONDON W4 3LT
☎ 0181-995 5332. PHONE FIRST.
All of the above are part of the British Equipment Hirers Association (BEHA), which has more than 100 members countrywide. A range of equipment can be hired from high chairs, cots and travel cots to baby car seats and buggies. Some members also hire out party equipment including child-sized tables and chairs. BEHA run an advice line which will try and answer any queries you have regarding hiring services for children. Phone the Babyline on 0831 310355.

CHELSEA BABY EQUIPMENT HIRE
51 LAMBERHURST ROAD, WEST NORWOOD,
LONDON SE27 0SD
☎ 0181-670 7304. BY APPOINTMENT ONLY.
Delivery and collection hire service for children's and nursery equipment including cots, prams, pushchairs, and swings. Some equipment is also for sale by this business which has been in operation for 10 years.

HARLEQUIN BABY HIRE

☎ 0171-704 0625. PHONE FOR BROCHURE.

Hires out baby equipment from prams and pushchairs to high chairs and car seats. Phone for brochure.

JANICE FRIEND

☎ 0181-952 2544. PHONE FIRST.

Cake tins in a variety of children's cake shapes – from Disney to Barbie doll – plus recipe sheets, for hire. Customers have to collect from her premises in Stanmore, Middlesex.

THE BABY'S ROOM

173 ST JOHN'S HILL, WANDSWORTH, LONDON SW11
☎ 0171-924 4711. OPEN 10 – 6 MON – SAT, 11 – 3 SUN.

Specialising in secondhand nursery equipment for infants and tiny tots up to the age of three, they also hire out cots, car seats, buggies, high chairs and prams.

Many women's magazines now have pages of freebies. For example, one issue of *Practical Parenting* offered £4,000-worth of free gifts including 100 videos worth £9.99 each, and 50 bathtime kits worth £15 each. If you really don't want to spend any money, nip into your local largest newsagent where you won't be spotted noting down the details and then send in your name and address and hope you strike lucky. The winners are usually picked at random after a set closing date.

SOUTH EAST

A & A BABY ACCESSORY HIRE
28 SWEPSTONE CLOSE, LOWER EARLY, READING, BERKSHIRE
RG6 3EE
☎ (01734) 669200. PHONE FIRST.

ABACUS BABY HIRE VALE FARM
WESTCOTT, DORKING, SURREY RH4 3LP
☎ (01306) 882242. PHONE FIRST.
6 NIGHTINGALE CRESCENT, WEST HORSLEY, SURREY
☎ (01486) 55142. PHONE FIRST.

ABC HIRE (CROYDON, SURREY)
☎ 0181-656 1342. PHONE FIRST.

BABES AND BUMPS
1 GILBY GREEN, NEAR SAFFRON WALDEN, NEWPORT,
ESSEX CB11 3RS
☎ (01799) 541978. PHONE FIRST.

BABY & CHILD EQUIPMENT HIRE
212 FINCHAMPSTEAD, WOKINGHAM, BERKSHIRE RG11 3HV
☎ (01734) 781463. PHONE FIRST.

BABYRENT (FRIMLEY)
80 PEVENSEY WAY, FRIMLEY, CAMBERLEY, SURREY
GU16 5UX
☎ (01252) 835638. PHONE FIRST.

BABYWARE HIRE
678 GALLEYWOOD ROAD, CHELMSFORD, ESSEX CM2 8BY
☎ (01245) 251666. PHONE FIRST.

BABYWISE HIRE
THE BAYS QUEENSWAY, HAYLING ISLAND, HAMPSHIRE
PO11 0LY
☎ (01705) 468385. PHONE FIRST.

BUGGIES PLUS
127 Smarts Lane, Loughton, Essex IG10 4BP
☎ 0181-508 8248. Phone First.

KID EQUIP
☎ (01737) 360448. Phone First.

KIDDYHIRE
6 Cooper Road, Croydon, Surrey CR0 4DL
☎ 0181-681 6443. Phone First.

KINDERHIRE
31 Kennedy Avenue, East Grinstead, West Sussex
RH19 2DH
☎ (01342) 322964. Phone First.
9 May Tree Close, Badger Farm, Winchester,
Hampshire SO22 4JB
☎ (01962) 863692. Phone First.

LIBERTY TRAVELLING TOTS
54 Foredown Drive, Portslade, Sussex BN41 2BE
☎ (01273) 422890. Phone First.

MOTHER GOOSE NURSERY HIRE
39 Lingfield Avenue, Kingston Upon Thames, Surrey
KT1 2TL
☎ 0181-541 1681. Phone First.

NURSERY HIRE
25 Necton Road, Wheathampstead, Hertfordshire
AL4 8AT
☎ (01582) 833904. Phone First.

NURSERY NEEDS (BIGGIN HILL, KENT)
☎ (01959) 540930. Phone First.

NURSERY & TODDLER SERVICES
67 Plantation Road, Leighton Buzzard, Bedfordshire
LU7 7HJ
☎ (01525) 378938. Phone First.

RASCALS BABY EQUIPMENT HIRE
16 PAYNE ROAD, WOOTTON, BEDFORDSHIRE MK43 9PJ
☎ (01234) 766931. PHONE FIRST.

ROBINA BABY & NURSERY EQUIPMENT
10 DOWNSWAY, SHOREHAM BY SEA, WEST SUSSEX
BN34 5GH
☎ (01273) 453548. PHONE FIRST.

ROCK-A-BYE
SUFFOLK HOUSE, THE GREEN, WOODBURN GREEN,
BUCKINGHAMSHIRE HP10 0EU
☎ (01628) 523159. PHONE FIRST.

ROCKABI
14 LOTHAIR ROAD, STOPSLEY, LUTON, BEDFORDSHIRE
LV2 7XB
☎ (01582) 455261. PHONE FIRST.

TINKERS
17 OLD OAK AVENUE, CHIPSTEAD, SURREY CR5 3PG
☎ (01737) 553761. PHONE FIRST.

TOTS 'N' TODDLERS
68 BEACON DRIVE, SEAFORD, EAST SUSSEX BN25 2JX
☎ (01323) 890962. PHONE FIRST.
All of the above are part of the British Equipment Hirers
Association (BEHA), which has more than 100 members
countrywide. A range of equipment can be hired from high
chairs, cots and travel cots to baby car seats and buggies. Some
members also hire out party equipment including child-sized
tables and chairs. BEHA run an advice line which will try and
answer any queries you have regarding hiring services for
children. Phone the Babyline on 0831 310355.

SOUTH WEST

ABACUS BABY EQUIPMENT HIRE
89 SEABOURNE ROAD, SOUTHBOURNE, BOURNEMOUTH,
DORSET BH8 9BJ
☎ (01202) 429829. PHONE FIRST.

BABE-EQUIP
9 LEAT STREET, TIVERTON, DEVON EX16 5LG
☎ (01884) 257938. PHONE FIRST.

BABY HIRE
35 LANGDON ROAD, BRADWORTHY, HOLSWORTHY, DEVON
EX22 7SF
☎ (01409) 241314. PHONE FIRST.

HUSH-A-BYE HIRE
16 WHITCHURCH AVENUE, EXETER, DEVON EX2 5NU
☎ (01392) 57636. PHONE FIRST.

JUST FOR YOU
9 TREMLETT MEWS, WORLE, WESTON SUPER MARE,
AVON BS22 0YL
☎ (01934) 510092. PHONE FIRST.

KINDER CARE
159 COWICK STREET, ST THOMAS, EXETER,
DEVON EX4 1AS
☎ (01392) 435888. PHONE FIRST.

LITTLE ONES NURSERY HIRE
24 PRESTBURY, YATE, BRISTOL, AVON BS17 4LB
☎ (01454) 325004. PHONE FIRST.

TRAVEL TOTS
2 BROADLEAS, KING EDWARD ROAD, MINEHEAD, SOMERSET
TA24 5JB
☎ (01643) 706213. PHONE FIRST.
All of the above are part of the British Equipment Hirers

Association (BEHA), which has more than 100 members countrywide. A range of equipment can be hired from high chairs, cots and travel cots to baby car seats and buggies. Some members also hire out party equipment including child-sized tables and chairs. BEHA run an advice line which will try and answer any queries you have regarding hiring services for children. Phone the Babyline on 0831 310355.

Buy a child's car seat from Kwik Fit and if returned in good condition, your money will be refunded. This is particularly useful for parents who opt for a car seat which only lasts until their baby is about nine months old, rather than a seat which can be used until the age of four or five, by which time it will almost certainly be too grubby to exchange. Check Yellow Pages for your local supplier.

WALES AND WEST MIDLANDS

LITTLE GEMS
20 COTEN END, WARWICKSHIRE CV34 4NP
☎ (01926) 408248. OPEN 10 – 5 MON – FRI,
10.30 – 4 SAT.
Nearly-new clothes and equipment for babies to twelve year olds with a hire service also offered.

ABC NURSERY
HIRE CONEY HALL, COLLETS GREEN, POWICK,
WORCESTERSHIRE WR2 4SB
☎ (01905) 830456. PHONE FIRST.

ANGLESEY NURSERY & TOY HIRE
10 GORWEL DEG, RHOSTREHWFA, LLANGEFNI, GWYNEDD
LL77 7JL
☎ (01248) 723181. PHONE FIRST.

BABY BOOM
96 NUFFIELD ROAD, COVENTRY, WEST MIDLANDS
CV6 7HW
☎ (01203) 666527. PHONE FIRST.

BABY BORROWS
4 ST JAMES VIEW, WANTAGE, OXFORDSHIRE OX12 0HT
☎ (01235) 868851. PHONE FIRST.

BABY HIRE
WYCHWOOD, NORTH BROOK ROAD, COVENTRY,
WARWICKSHIRE CV6 2AJ
☎ (01203) 334787. PHONE FIRST.

BABY LINES
SUNNYRIDGE, LUSTON, LEOMINSTER, HEREFORDSHIRE
HR6 0EB
☎ (01568) 612357. PHONE FIRST.

CHUCKLES BABY HIRE
THE GRANARY, HALF KEY COURT, MALVERN,
WORCESTERSHIRE WR14 1UP
☎ (01886) 833594. PHONE FIRST.

HOME AND AWAY
50 ELM GROVE, BROMSGROVE, WORCESTERSHIRE B61 0EJ
☎ (01527) 875188. PHONE FIRST.

IMPS BABY EQUIPMENT HIRE
18 ST MARY'S ROAD, BEARWOOD, WARLEY, WEST
MIDLANDS B67 5DG
☎ (0121) 420 3266. PHONE FIRST.

IMPS NURSERY HIRE
CHURCH FARM, NEW CHURCH, BURTON ON TRENT,
STAFFORDSHIRE DE13 8RJ
☎ (01283) 75372. PHONE FIRST.
3 MAIN STREET, STAPENHILL, BURTON ON TRENT,
STAFFORDSHIRE DE15 9AP
☎ (01238) 511822. PHONE FIRST.

KIDDICARE
24 OAKDENE ROAD, HEMEL HEMPSTEAD, HERTFORDSHIRE
HP3 9TS
☎ (01442) 214559. PHONE FIRST.

KINDERHIRE LTD
7 BEDINGSTONE DRIVE, STAFFORD, PENKRIDGE,
STAFFORDSHIRE ST19 5TE
☎ (01785) 715060. PHONE FIRST.

LITTLE MONKEYS
4 HOLLOWFIELDS CLOSE, REDDITCH, WORCESTERSHIRE
B98 7NR
☎ (01527) 550988. PHONE FIRST.

MERCIA SAFEY CENTRE
3 SLADE HILL, HAMPTON MAGNA, NEAR WARWICK,
WARWICKSHIRE CV35 8JA
☎ (01926) 411388. PHONE FIRST.

MOLD NURSERY HIRE

HAWTHORNS, LLYN-Y-PANDY LANE, MOLD,
CLYWD CH7 5JF
☎ (01352) 740250. PHONE FIRST.

NOW AND THEN

1 LLYS TUDUR, PARK VIEW, RHYL, CLWYD LL18 4AX
☎ (01745) 332530. PHONE FIRST.

SMALL TALK EQUIPMENT HIRE

204 OLD BATH ROAD, CHELTENHAM, GLOUCESTERSHIRE
GL53 9EQ
☎ (01242) 231902. OPEN 9 – 5 SEVEN DAYS A WEEK.

THURSDAYS CHILD

3 OAKWOOD CLOSE, ESSINGTON, WOLVERHAMPTON,
WEST MIDLANDS WV11 2DQ
☎ (01922) 402010. PHONE FIRST.

TOGS FOR TOTS

LONGACRE HOUSE, NESSCLIFFE, SHREWSBURY, SHROPSHIRE
SY4 1BJ
☎ (01743) 81335. PHONE FIRST.

All of the above are part of the British Equipment Hirers
Association (BEHA), which has more than 100 members
countrywide. A range of equipment can be hired from high
chairs, cots and travel cots to baby car seats and buggies. Some
members also hire out party equipment including child-sized
tables and chairs. BEHA run an advice line which will try and
answer any queries you have regarding hiring services for
children. Phone the Babyline on 0831 310355.

EAST ANGLIA AND EAST MIDLANDS

ABBEY NURSERY HIRE

183C DUFFIELD ROAD, DARLEY ABBEY, DERBY, DERBYSHIRE
DE22 1JB
☎ (01332) 558766. PHONE FIRST.

ABSOLUTE BEGINNERS

162 RADCLIFFE ROAD, WEST BRIDGFORD, NOTTINGHAM,
NOTTINGHAMSHIRE NG2 5HF
☎ (0115) 9818135. PHONE FIRST.

BABY RENT

14 THE BOLTONS, SOUTH WOOTTON, KING'S LYNN,
NORFOLK PE30 3NQ ·
☎ (01553) 674200. OPEN WEEKDAY EVES, SOME
MORNINGS, SAT MORNINGS, PHONE FIRST.

CUDDLES NURSERY HIRE

1A PARKWAY, WESTON FAVELL, NORTHAMPTON,
NORTHAMPTONSHIRE NN3 3BS
☎ (01604) 411233. OPEN 10 – 3 TUE, 9 – 12 WED,
9 – 5 THUR, SAT, 9 – 5.30 MON, FRI.
Specialises in car seats, enabling the parent to try the child in
the car seat first, and emphasising the safety angle. Minimum
hire is for six months and costs from £9.50 to £19.50 depending
on the model. Cuddles also hires out travel cots, christening
wear, high chairs, pushchairs and backpacks. Minimum hire is
for four nights. The customer has to pick up the items. Cuddles
also sells a full range of nursery equipment, either new or
former hire, and a range of broderie anglaise and satin
christening wear from £15–£45. Part of the British Equipment
Hirers Association (BEHA), which has more than 100 members
countrywide. BEHA run an advice line which will try and

answer any queries you have regarding hiring services for children. Phone the Babyline on 0831 310355.

NIKKIS NURSERY HIRE

1 RECTORY FARM COTTAGE, ROOKERY ROAD, STRETTON OAKHAM, RUTLAND LE15 7RA
☎ (01780) 410359. PHONE FIRST.

NURSERY HIRE

FIELD COTTAGE, MARCH LANE, FELIXSTOWE, SUFFOLK IP11 9RW
☎ (01394) 282351. PHONE FIRST.

PLAYSAFE NURSERY HIRE

14 BELMONT DRIVE, COALVILLE, LEICESTERSHIRE LE67 3LQ
☎ (01530) 831119. PHONE FIRST.
2A SWANNINGTON ROAD, RAVENSTONE, LEICESTERSHIRE LE67 3NE
☎ (01530) 813136. PHONE FIRST.

TINY TRAVELLERS B.E. HIRE

54 ANDREW GOODALL CLOSE, TOFTWOOD, DEREHAM, NORFOLK NR19 1SR
☎ (01362) 697150. PHONE FIRST.

If you're pregnant, don't forget that you are eligible for free dental treatment and prescriptions up to one year after the birth of your baby. You'll also be given free booklets on parenthood by your health visitor or ante natal clinic.

NORTH WEST, YORKSHIRE AND HUMBERSIDE

BABY DAYS
27 DOWER PARK, ESRICK, YORK, NORTH YORKSHIRE
YO4 6JN
☎ (01904) 728158. PHONE FIRST.

BABY EQUIPMENT HIRE
1 PEEBLES CLOSE, LITTLE SUTTON, SOUTH WIRRAL,
LANCASHIRE L66 4JX
☎ (0151) 348 0620. PHONE FIRST.

BOUNCING BABIES
167 TOTTINGTON ROAD, HARWOOD, BOLTON, LANCASHIRE
BL2 4DF
☎ (01204) 302762. PHONE FIRST.

CHESHIRE BABY HIRE
9 RYDAL CLOSE, HOLMES CHAPEL, CHESHIRE CW4 7JR
☎ (01477) 533414. PHONE FIRST.
BROADWAY FARM, TWEMLOW, NEAR HOLMES CHAPEL,
CHESHIRE
☎ (01477) 71237. PHONE FIRST.

DEJA VU
134 NORTHENDEN ROAD, SALE MOOR, CHESHIRE M33 3HE
☎ (0161) 969 5495. PHONE FIRST.

HICCUPS
38 HEATHER LEE AVENUE, DORE, SHEFFIELD,
SOUTH YORKSHIRE S17 3DL
☎ (0114) 2366054. PHONE FIRST.

HIRE IT FOR BABY
PARTRIDGE HILL FARM, AUSTERFIELD, DONCASTER,
SOUTH YORKSHIRE DN10 6HA
☎ (01302) 711873. PHONE FIRST.

JACK AND JILL

38 PARKWAYS GROVE, LEEDS, WEST YORKSHIRE LS26 8TP
☎ (01532) 828323. PHONE FIRST.
85 SANDHILL OVAL, ALWOODLEY, LEEDS, WEST YORKSHIRE
LS17 8EF
☎ (0113) 2683712. PHONE FIRST.
566 WAKEFIELD ROAD, HUDDERSFIELD, WEST YORKSHIRE
HD5 8PU
☎ (01484) 530486. PHONE FIRST.
1 WEST PARK DRIVE, WEST PARK, LEEDS, WEST YORKSHIRE
LS16 5AS
☎ (01532) 785560. PHONE FIRST.
5 CARLTON LANE, GUISELEY, LEEDS, WEST YORKSHIRE
LS20 2DB
☎ (01943) 877637.

KIDDYHIRE

1 WHIN GROVE, BOLTON LE SANDS, LANCASTER,
LANCASHIRE LA5 8DD
☎ (01524) 734136. PHONE FIRST.
4 WESTFIELD GROVE, WAKEFIELD, WEST YORKSHIRE
WF1 2RS
☎ (01924) 365732. PHONE FIRST.

MOTHER GOOSE NURSERY EQUIPMENT

1 WHITWELL TERRACE, MELMERBY, RIPON, NORTH
YORKSHIRE HG4 5HQ
☎ (01765) 640443. PHONE FIRST.

NORTH WEST BABY HIRE

1 SIDE AVENUE, ATTRINGHAM, CHESHIRE WA14 3AP
☎ (0161) 941 4916. PHONE FIRST.

NURSERY NEEDS

43 PIKEPURSE LANE, RICHMOND, NORTH YORKSHIRE
DL10 4PS
☎ (01748) 824524. PHONE FIRST.

NURSERY TIMES HIRE

19 Edinburgh Place, Leeds, West Yorkshire LS25 2LN
☎ (0113) 2875321. Phone First.

RAINBOW

Station Road, Oakworth, Keighley, West Yorkshire
BD22 0DV
☎ 01535 644433. Phone First.
20 Dockray Street, Colne, Lancashire
☎ 01282 869141. Phone First.

All of the above are part of the British Equipment Hirers Association (BEHA), which has more than 100 members countrywide. A range of equipment can be hired from high chairs, cots and travel cots to baby car seats and buggies. Some members also hire out party equipment including child-sized tables and chairs. BEHA run an advice line which will try and answer any queries you have regarding hiring services for children. Phone the Babyline on 0831 310355.

MILUPA BABYFOOD

Scientific Department, Milupa House, Uxbridge
Road, Hillingdon, Middlesex UB10 0NE
☎ 0181-573 9966.

About to wean your baby? Test his or her taste buds without opening your purse. Write to Milupa, who produce baby foods, with the date of birth of your infant, and they will send you free samples at a time that is appropriate to your baby's age.

NORTH AND SCOTLAND

A & E COOPER
Marhaba, Sunnybank Road, St Ola, Orkney
KW15 1TP
☎ (01856) 874065. Phone First.

ABC BABY EQUIPMENT HIRE
9 Woodburn Avenue, Kilwinning, Ayrshire KA13 7DB
☎ (01294) 552549. Phone First.

BABY EQUIPMENT HIRE
23 Willow Grove, Pitcorthie, Dunfermline, Fife,
Scotland KY11 5BB
☎ (01383) 720711. Phone First.

BABY BABY EQUIPMENT HIRE
5 Cammo Brae, Edinburgh, Scotland EH4 8ET
☎ (0131) 339 5215. Phone First.

BABY NEST
222 Marshall Wallis Road, South Shields,
Tyne & Wear NE33 5PW
☎ (0191) 455 9937. Phone First.

BABY WORLD
84 North Bridge Street, Bathgate, West Lothian
EH48 1DE
☎ (01506) 56318. Phone First.

BOBTAILS ROSE COTTAGE
Kessock, Inverness, Scotland IV1 1XG
☎ (01463) 731739. Phone First.

BUCKSTONE BABY HIRE
22 Buckstone Circle, Edinburgh, Scotland EH10 6XB
☎ (0131) 445 2825. Phone First.

COT CO
45 COPTLEIGH, HOUGHTON LE SPRING,
TYNE & WEAR DH5 8JE
☎ (0191) 512 0242. PHONE FIRST.

KIDS STUFF
5 LOVAINE TERRACE, BERWICK-ON-TWEED,
NORTHUMBERLAND TD15 1LA
☎ (01289) 307208. PHONE FIRST.

ROCK-A-BYE BABY
8 ACADEMY GARDENS, GAINFORD, DURHAM DL2 3EN
☎ (01325) 730773. PHONE FIRST.
25 LARUN BEAT, YARM, CLEVELAND TS15 9HP
☎ (01642) 785352. PHONE FIRST.

SHUFFLES
MORVEN, FERNTOWER ROAD, CRIEFF, PERTHSHIRE PH7 3BX
☎ (01764) 654835. PHONE FIRST.

TINY TOTS HIRE
KIRKLAND FARM, LESWALT, BY STRANRAER,
WIGTOWNSHIRE
☎ (01776) 870214. PHONE FIRST.

WESTFIELD
1 WILLOWDENE CRES, STRANRAER, WIGTOWNSHIRE
DG9 0HE
☎ (01776) 703894. PHONE FIRST.

All of the above are part of the British Equipment Hirers
Association (BEHA), which has more than 100 members
countrywide. A range of equipment can be hired from high
chairs, cots and travel cots to baby car seats and buggies. Some
members also hire out party equipment including child-sized
tables and chairs. BEHA run an advice line which will try and
answer any queries you have regarding hiring services for
children. Phone the Babyline on 0831 310355.

BABY BABY EQUIPMENT HIRE

45 GLENDEVON PLACE, EDINBURGH EH12 5UH
☎ 0131-337 7016. SEVEN DAYS A WEEK. PHONE FIRST.
A member of the Baby Equipment Hirers Association (BEHA), a nationwide referral service with its own code of conduct, Baby Baby hires out all types of equipment from prams to cots. Travel cots cost from £10 for one week's hire, high chairs £15 for a fortnight. No minimum time necessary, although it is obviously cheaper to hire for a longer period. For example, hiring a car seat for one week costs £10 but for three months the cost would only be £30. Equipment is not sold off and there is no membership fee. There is a standard delivery charge of £5 within the city and a collection charge of £2–£5 depending on where the customer lives.

IMMACULATE

72 HAYMARKET TERRACE, EDINBURGH, SCOTLAND
☎ (0131) 346 4242. OPEN 9.30 – 5 MON – SAT,
UNTIL 6.30 ON THUR.
Boys' formal wear as well as men's dinner suits and Highland outfits for hire.

KIT FOR KIDS

5 COLLINS CLOSE, KENDAL, CUMBRIA LA9 5JF
☎ (01539) 723293.
Caters mostly for short term requirements, hiring out travel cots, high chairs, playpens and car seats, all the equipment needed for children 0–8 years old. Car seats cost £8 per week, travel cots, £10. Deposits of between £10–£30 are required. Local deliveries are free; those up to 20 miles away cost £10. There is a high turnover of merchandise and most ex-hire equipment is sold off at regular periods. As we went to press, the business was for sale but all calls will be passed on to the new owner.

McCALLS OF THE ROYAL MILE
11 THE HIGH STREET, EDINBURGH EH1 1SR
☎ (0131) 557 3979. OPEN 9 – 5.30 MON – WED, SAT,
9 – 7.30 THUR, FRI, 12 – 4 SUN.
Hire and sell men's formal wear, and boys' outfits, but not girls'.

TURNABOUT
32 PRIORY PLACE, CRAIGIE, PERTH, SCOTLAND
☎ (01738) 630916. OPEN 9.30 – 5 MON – FRI, 10 – 4 SAT.
Nearly-new children's clothes shop which also hires out
equipment from high chairs, cots, prams and buggies to
playpens and car seats.

NORTHERN IRELAND

ECONOMY BABY HIRE

67 CLONTONACALLY ROAD, CASTLEREAGH, BELFAST,
COUNTY DOWN BT6 9SJ
☎ (01232) 448657. PHONE FIRST.

Part of the British Equipment Hirers Association (BEHA), which has more than 100 members countrywide. A range of equipment can be hired from high chairs, cots and travel cots to baby car seats and buggies. Some members also hire out party equipment including child-sized tables and chairs. BEHA run an advice line which will try and answer any queries you have regarding hiring services for children. Phone the Babyline on 0831 310355.